T0274551

1939

1939

Jani Lauzon and Kaitlyn Riordan

1939
first published 2024 by Scirocco Drama
An imprint of J. Gordon Shillingford Publishing Inc.
© 2024 Jani Lauzon and Kaitlyn Riordan

The quotation on page 69 is from a poem by Louis Riel titled "Je ne suis pas de ceuz qui cherchent les ruines" published in *The Collected Writings of Louis Riel / Les Ecrits Complets de Louis Riel*, George Stanley, Raymond Huel, Gilles Martel, Thomas Flanagan, and Glen Campbell, Eds. (1985). Reprinted by permission of the publisher, University of Alberta Press (Edmonton.)

The quotations on page 42 and 46 are from *The Story of My Life* by Ellen Terry, first published by Hutchinson & Co, London, 1900.

"1939" Reflections on Adaptation, Indigenous Theatre, and Shakespeare's Legacy: An interview with Jani Lauzon and Kaitlyn Riordan, interview by Sorouja Moll, is reprinted from *Canadian Theatre Review* Volume 197, Winter 2024 with the permission of CTR. DOI:10.3138/ctr.197.024

Scirocco Drama Editor: Glenda MacFarlane
Cover design by Doowah Design
Author photo of Jani Lauzon by Denise Grant
Author photo of Kaitlyn Riordan by Sam Gaetz
Production photos by David Hou

Printed and bound in Canada on 100% post-consumer recycled paper.

Production inquiries to:
kaitlynriordan12@gmail.com

Library and Archives Canada Cataloguing in Publication

Title: 1939 / Jani Lauzon and Kaitlyn Riordan.
Other titles: Nineteen thirty-nine
Names: Lauzon, Jani, author. | Riordan, Kaitlyn, author.
Description: Previously published: Toronto, ON: Playwrights Guild of Canada, 2023.
Identifiers: Canadiana 20240455053 | ISBN 9781990738623 (softcover)
Subjects: LCGFT: Drama.
Classification: LCC PS8623.A8333 A15 2024 | DDC C812/.6—dc23

We acknowledge the financial support of the Canada Council for the Arts, the Government of Canada, the Manitoba Arts Council, and the Manitoba Government for our publishing program.

J. Gordon Shillingford Publishing
P.O. Box 86, RPO Corydon Avenue, Winnipeg, MB Canada R3M 3S3

To the memory of Elder Pauline Shirt

Jani Lauzon

Jani Lauzon is a nominated actor/writer/director, a Juno-nominated singer/songwriter, and a Gemini Award–winning puppeteer. Her company, Paper Canoe Projects, was created to support production of her own work including: *A Side of Dreams, I Call myself Princess,* and *Prophecy Fog.* Previous writing includes: *The Scrubbing Project, The Triple Truth,* and *The Only Good Indian* with Turtle Gals Performance Ensemble. She has been playwright-in-residence at Cahoots Theatre Projects and Factory Theatre. Other residencies include: The Tracey Wright Global Archive at The Theatre Centre, Nightswimming Theatre, and the Barker Fairly Distinguished Writer-in-Residence Fellowship. Jani was the Senior Playwright-in-Residence at the Banff Playwrights Colony in April 2015. www.janilauzon.com; www.papercanoeprojects.com.

Kaitlyn Riordan

Kaitlyn Riordan is an actor/playwright of Irish and French descent. She was part of the leadership team at Shakespeare in the Ruff from 2012 to 2021. There, her play, *Portia's Julius Caesar*, premièred in 2018 and was later produced at Hart House Theatre, the University of Waterloo, and by the Little Lion Theatre in Stratford-Upon-Avon and in London, UK. *1939*, which she co-wrote with Jani Lauzon, premièred at The Stratford Festival in 2022 and was short-listed for the Carol Bolt Award by the Playwrights Guild of Canada. Plays in development include *Gertrude's Hamlet, I Sit Content—a story of Emily Carr,* and *The Nude Nun*. Kaitlyn is a four-time Dora Mavor Moore Award nominee for acting. www.kaitlynriordan.com

Acknowledgements

Jani Lauzon and Kaitlyn Riordan are members of the Playwrights Guild of Canada.

1939 was originally commissioned by the Stratford Festival, Ontario, Canada. Special thank you to Shakespeare in the Ruff which, through the Canada Council, helped support the initial script development.

The playwrights wish to thank the following for their support in the development of 1939:

Antoni Cimolino, Anita Gaffney, Keira Loughran, ted witzel and Rachel Wormsbecher from the Stratford Festival; Eva Barrie and AJ Richardson from Shakespeare in the Ruff; Rev. Dr. Stephen Drakeford and Nancy Hern from the Anglican Church of Canada and its archives, Krista McCracken from the Algoma University archives, Rebecca Burton from The Playwrights Guild of Canada, Keith Barker, Jessica Carmichael, Waawaate Fobister, Roger Fobister Sr., David Mildon, Sorouja Moll, Yvette Nolan, and Minnie Akparook. And most importantly our Elder Script Consultants: Pauline Shirt, Shirley Horn, Edna Manitowabi, Elizabeth Stevens.

The playwrights would also like to thank the actors and stage managers who participated in the development of 1939 between 2018 and 2022; Marion Adler, Brendan Chandler, Kat Chin, Richard Comeau, Sarah Dodd, Deborah Drakeford, Sheldon Elter, Jacklyn Francis, Renate Hanson, Robert Harding, Braiden Houle, Nicole Joy-Fraser, Madison Kalbhenn, Wahsonti:io Kirby, Shira Leuchter, Cheri Maracle, Kathleen MacLean, Brendan McMurtry-Howlett, Jeff Meadows, Chris Mejaki, Lisa Nasson, Joelle Peters, Gregory Prest, Mike Shara, Tara Sky, James Dallas Smith, Aqua Nibii Waawaaskone, John Wamsley, and Gordon Patrick White.

Playwrights' Notes

In June of 2024, I travelled to Sault St. Marie with a group of actors from various productions to do a staged reading of *1939* for the Children of Shingwauk Alumni Association. Survivors of the Shingwauk Residential School, along with their families, gathered outside on a beautiful sunny day to listen to our play. Shirley Horn, who Kaitlyn and I worked with while writing the play, planted the seed for this many years ago and thanks to YES! Theatre and the CSAA we finally made it happen. The experience was, to say the least, profound.

I won't lie. I was nervous. We are telling their story. We have never taken that responsibility lightly. But to have the Survivors there, smiling, laughing, crying, wow. It brings tears to my eyes even now seeing them in my mind, Shirley Horn, Jackie Fletcher, John Saylors, Daisy, Irene, George, Dolly, and many others who came to listen and then feast with us and share their stories. These are stories of strength, tenacity, resilience and the most incredible courage. They have worked hard all their lives to overcome, to find peace, love, self-acceptance, after experiencing unspeakable things. Their strength humbled me and reminded me of why doing this work is important. Kaitlyn and I did ceremony while writing this play. I prayed that our story would be medicine. As Jay Jones, President of the Children of Shingwauk Association says about the work of healing and reconciliation, "There's no game plan to do this kind of work. We have to do this in a loving, caring, healing way." I am profoundly grateful to be able to offer, in the spirit of reconciliation, this medicine, our play, to those who deserve and need it the most and to those who understand the importance of embracing the history of this country in its entirety.

—*Jani Lauzon, Spring 2024*

My son is five months old today. On our daily walks, I see children of all ages coming home from school and imagine him doing the same one day. I do so with joy, daydreaming of the things he'll learn and the friends he'll make. At no point do I think about him being taken away from me and shipped off to another part of the country, of being forced to learn a language I can't speak, of being taught that our way of life is wrong. Just imagining this scenario is painful. That so many Indigenous parents lived it, and much worse, is unthinkable.

When Justice Murray Sinclair presented the findings of the Truth and Reconciliation Commission (TRC) of Canada in 2015, I was dumbfounded. I wondered how I'd missed such a vital lesson in school; certain that the amazing school I attended hadn't neglected to teach it. It couldn't have, not such an important element of our national story; one that has so negatively impacted so many lives and one that has profoundly altered my relationship to my citizenship. The work of the TRC was a call to action for me to take that learning upon myself.

Very quickly, I discovered that there was an abundance of teachers to be found. Many had written books about their experiences, agreed to be filmed while sharing their stories, created works of art, were helping their communities heal, and leading those willing to listen on the path of reconciliation. I count myself profoundly graced that this path eventually led me to meeting Jani Lauzon.

Jani is an artist of profound integrity and a collaborator whom I cherish. I have been changed by the experience we undertook of researching and writing this play and feel very lucky that storytelling is where I was able to funnel that energy.

In the 83rd Call to Action of the TRC's final report, they call upon the Canada Council for the Arts to establish, as a funding priority, a strategy for Indigenous and non-Indigenous artists to undertake collaborative projects and produce works that contribute to the reconciliation process. This guided our work and encouraged me, as a non-Indigenous artist, to imagine how I could participate. This is not an uncomplicated thing to contemplate, but I have come to understand that we silo the history of our shared land at a grave price. The genocide that occurred through the Residential School system and the Indian Act is incumbent on all of us to reckon with, just as reconciliation must be as well.

My greatest ambition in co-writing *1939* was to honour Survivors and those who didn't survive, with the hopes of contributing to the process of reconciliation. These are lofty ambitions and ones that I carry forward with me as I envision what it means to be a parent and an artist on this land today.

—*Kaitlyn Riordan, Spring 2024*

Foreword

It is both an honour and a privilege to be asked to write this foreword for this incredible work by Jani Lauzon and Kaitlyn Riordan, both very talented and dedicated artists. Residential Schools, for the many children that passed through their doors, meant more than simply being within the walls of an institution. Not only physically, but mentally and spiritually, these schools resulted in long-lasting impacts on us, our families, and whole communities.

1939 is a play that shows the many facets of what we faced on a daily basis. We were always under scrutiny from our supervisors and priests, who constantly threatened punishment for talking, looking at each other, being in the wrong place at the wrong time. It seemed there was nothing we could do to avoid the wrath of the powers-that-be.

I must admit that the idea of children performing a Shakespearean play for the King of England is ridiculous! Before coming to the school, the students would have never heard of Shakespeare. The irony was that we were not allowed to speak our own languages, yet we were expected to be able to understand the strange-sounding English language that was so different from our own. We often took a beating because we didn't understand what was being said.

The chosen students within the play were willing to study and learn because it offered them a chance to interact with each other and share a feeling of closeness and family, something that was very rare in the cold institutional environment. We were very cautious about secret moments we stole, daring to speak with each other and letting our feelings slip into our conversations under threat of punishment if we were caught. Throughout the play these moments were well placed and meaningful, with fear being the overarching emotion of institutional life.

1939 highlights the resilience of the children and the way we met the many challenges in spite of the difficulty of what was expected of us. This was a common theme that we dealt with over and over again in our day-to-day life in Residential Schools. We all had to find a way to accept our situation and make the best of it until we left the school for summer vacation, or permanently when we came of age.

Not all experiences were terrible. Some of us had some good experiences that left us with gifts that stayed with us for our lifetimes. For me, one such gift was how one supervisor shared her love of classical music with us. As we were getting ready for church on Sunday mornings, she would leave her room door open as she played music on her record player, which allowed us to hear and enjoy the wonderful opera themes and Strauss waltzes which I still love today. She probably never knew how much I enjoyed it. I count this experience as among the most treasured moments of my youth, and it has stayed with me throughout my life.

One of the most important actions that we as former students of Residential Schools undertook was to organize ourselves and start to gather the stories of former students, to begin to build an archive that holds these stories, pictures, and memorabilia. We also still bring former students together to meet to share stories and healing through conversation, circles, and traditional ceremonies. The group is called The Children of Shingwauk Alumni Association (CSAA) and has successfully been doing this work since 1981. It has helped us start to address the trauma of the aftermath of the Residential School era.

Organizations sprang into action to find their place in addressing these atrocities and asked, "How can we help?" What could be done to help repair the damage and restore "what was taken away"? Many groups met and talked about what they could do to bring about healing in the spirit of Truth and Reconciliation. We identified ways through studies, group activities, and the gathering of information by churches and government, as they were called to accountability under the Truth and Reconciliation agenda.

Others are very much a part of the healing and restorative movement, especially First Nation artists who themselves, their families, and communities have been impacted by traumatic Residential School experiences. Many authors of books on the subject have contributed to making the stories known throughout the world. Visual artists, with their paintings, have told about the suffering of the children, very often with tragic conclusions. Storytellers, like the creators of *1939*, have contributed to spreading awareness through plays and working with Indigenous actors, some of whose own family members had experienced life in the Residential Schools.

My interest in the arts started at a very young age, when in my class I was often chosen to decorate the chalkboard with Christmas and holiday themes, as I had shown an aptitude for drawing and colouring. I thoroughly enjoyed this activity and regarded this time as very special in my life; it was a time when I felt valued and was allowed to express myself through art. In later years, encouraged by my love of art, I chose to attend university to study art and learn what I could about the fundamentals of drawing, painting and other artistic endeavours. I was successful in attaining a Bachelor of Fine Arts Degree, which gave me a great sense of accomplishment. During my studies I noticed that my art concentrated on my experiences at the school. I guess this was part of my own healing journey, which is ongoing in my life. This is the reason that I share my story when I am asked by educational institutions, mainstream groups, churches, gatherings of First Nation communities, celebrations and many other events that choose to facilitate healing for our people using traditional ways and ceremonies—which were denied our people for a century or more. We all need healing, and the arts are a very important part of that journey. The efforts put forward by the many artists go a long way to bring about healing for all. *1939* is one such segment of the healing agenda, and it is done with care and consideration to "get it right" in the spirit of Truth and Reconciliation.

The work carried out by everyone involved in this healing journey takes many forms and cannot be done alone, as the load is too heavy. Many hands and many minds are needed. The Children of Shingwauk Alumni Association works tirelessly with many partners, such as Algoma University, to find ways to support artists. The Anglican Church, First Nation groups, the city of Sault Ste Marie, the Stratford Festival, and other agencies, as well as the federal government, have all contributed to this noble cause.

We must keep telling the stories to bring about healing and understanding and to eventually be successful in the healing of our people and of bringing back "what was taken away" through Truth and Reconciliation.

Many thanks to *1939* and its role in telling the story.

—*Shirley Horn, Spring 2024*

Shirley Horn is the co-founder of Children of Shingwauk Alumni Association, served as the first Chancellor of Algoma University, and is the former Chief of the Missanabie Cree First Nation.

Production History

The première production opened on September 11, 2022 at the Studio Theatre, Stratford Festival. Antoni Cimolino, Artistic Director and Anita Gaffney, Executive Director.

Cast

Susan Blackbird	Kathleen MacLean
Sian Ap Dafydd	Sarah Dodd
Jean Delorme	John Wamsley
Madge Macbeth	Jacklyn Francis
Evelyne Rice	Wahsonti:io Kirby
Beth Summers	Tara Sky
Joseph Summers	Richard Comeau
Father Callum Williams	Mike Shara

Creative Team:

Director	Jani Lauzon
Set Designer	Joanna Yu
Lighting Designer	Louise Guinand
Costume Designer	Asa Benally
Sound Designer	Wayne Kelso
Dramaturge	Jessica Carmichael with ted witzel
Research Dramaturge	Sorouja Moll
Assistant Director	desirée leverenz
Assistant Designer	Victoria Spain

Assistant Lighting Designer .... Hannah Kirby

Assistant Sound Designer .... Olivia Wheeler

Stage Manager .... Bona Duncan

Assistant Stage Manager .... Ada Aguilar

Assistant Stage Manager .... Ken James Stewart

Anishinaabemowin Translations................ Waawaate
Fobister with Roger Fobister Sr.

Kanien'kéha Translations .... Wahsonti:io Kirby

Consulting Elder, Stratford Festival............. Elizabeth
Stevens

A subsequent production of *1939*, produced by YES! Theatre, opened on March 15, 2024.

Cast

Susan Blackbird .... Sarah Gartshore

Sian Ap Dafydd .... Deborah Drakeford

Jean Delorme .... Mackenzie Wójcik

Madge Macbeth .... Katie Wise

Evelyne Rice .... Lisa Cromarty

Beth Summers .... Kelsey Tyson

Joseph Summers .... Richard Comeau

Father Callum Williams .... Jake Deeth

Creative Team:

Director .... Jani Lauzon

Set Designer .... Diandra Zafiris

Lighting Designer .... Frank Donato

Costume Designer .... Christine Williston

Sound Designer .... Wayne Kelso

Assistant Costume Designer /
Head of Wardrobe .... Aurora Judge

Stage Manager .... Morgan Cook

Assistant Stage Manager .... Mikey Lampman

Assistant Stage Manager ....James Saxby

Elder Nokomis ....Martina Osawamick

Indigenous Arts & Cultural
Advisor (IACA) .... Will Morin

A Canadian Stage and Belfry Theatre joint production of *1939*, in association with The Stratford Festival, is scheduled for the fall of 2024, with the Canadian Stage production scheduled to open on September 19, 2024 and the Belfry Theatre, scheduled to open on October 31, 2024, with the following cast and creative team:

Cast

Susan Blackbird ....Brefny Caribou

Sian Ap Dafydd ....Catherine Fitch

Jean Delorme .... John Wamsley

Madge Macbeth .... Amanda Lisman

Evelyne Rice ....Merewyn Comeau

Beth Summers ....Grace Lamarche

Joseph Summers ....Richard Comeau

Father Callum Williams.........................Nathan Howe

Creative Team

Director .... Jani Lauzon

Set Designer ....Joanna Yu

Lighting Designer .... Louise Guinand

Costume Designer ....Asa Benally

Head of Wardrobe ....Janet Pym

Sound Designer ....Wayne Kelso

Stage Manager ....Sarah Miller

Assistant Stage Manager ....Maya Bowers

Associate Costume Designer ....Barbara Morrone-Sanchez

Associate Set Designer..................................Sim Suzer

Associate Lighting Designer................Sruthi Suresan

Cultural and Spiritual Advisor........Kelly Fran Davis

Richard Comeau (centre) as Joseph Summers with (from left) Tara Sky, John Wamsley, Kathleen MacLean and Wahsonti:io Kirby in *1939*, Stratford Festival 2022. Photo by David Hou.

From left: Tara Sky as Beth Summers, John Wamsley as Jean Delorme, Richard Comeau as Joseph Summers and Wahsonti:io Kirby as Evelyne Rice in *1939*, Stratford Festival 2022. Photo by David Hou.

From left: Wahsonti:io Kirby, Tara Sky and Kathleen MacLean in *1939*, Stratford Festival 2022. Photo by David Hou.

From left: Sarah Dodd, Wahsonti:io Kirby, Jacklyn Francis, Mike Shara in *1939*, Stratford Festival 2022. Photo by David Hou.

Tara Sky as Beth Summers in *1939*, Stratford Festival 2022. Photo by David Hou.

John Wamsley and members of the company in *1939*, Stratford Festival 2022. Photo by David Hou.

Tara Sky (left) as Beth Summers and Sarah Dodd as Sian Ap Dafydd in *1939*, Stratford Festival 2022. Photo by David Hou.

Tara Sky as Beth Summers and Richard Comeau as Joseph Summers in *1939*, Stratford Festival 2022. Photo by David Hou.

Characters

Susan Blackbird: Cree student, 16 years old

Sian Ap Dafydd: English teacher, Welsh descent, 50 years old

Jean Delorme: Algonquin Métis student, 16 years old

Madge Macbeth (based on a historical figure): Journalist, American-born, of English and Jewish descent, preferably an actor in their 60s

Evelyne Rice: Mohawk student, 16 years old

Beth Summers: Ojibwe student, 15 years old

Joseph Summers: Ojibwe former student, 17 years old

Callum Williams: Anglican Priest, English descent, and teacher, mid 30s

Notes on the Text

/ indicates beginning of overlapping dialogue.

— indicates the speaker was interrupted.

Setting

The play takes place in a fictional Residential School in northern Ontario. Although there are multiple locations in the play, the setting is primarily made up of three *oversized* chalkboards. There are also wooden chairs in two piles. If possible, pieces of broken chairs hang together above the stage to represent the spirits of the children who didn't survive.

Production Notes

During scene transitions, students write what is important to them on the chalkboards and various characters erase those images/words. This action represents erasure. They are not considered scenes but are included by the playwrights to indicate their importance. The content of these transitions from the world première at the Stratford Festival is included in this draft, though may not serve subsequent productions.

Throughout the course of the play, images also magically appear and disappear on these chalkboards. These images are referred to as "spirit images" in the stage directions. For the world première these images were made up of six pictographs. The authors recommend connecting with Knowledge Keepers in your area to obtain teachings and permission to use pictographs and/or images from petroglyphs.

As a general rule, the students raise their hands before asking questions until the convention has been established.

When text is spoken in a language other than English, the translation is included after the text in parenthesies and italics *(like this)*. It is not meant to be spoken but is there for clarity.

The Shakespearean text in this draft uses the punctuation, capitalization, and some spelling from the First Folio edition of *All's Well That Ends Well*, etc. Where the Elizabethan editors used one letter in the place of another (e.g., u instead of v), the playwrights chose spelling for clarity and went against the First Folio.

ACT I

Scene 1.1

We hear the sound of cadet-style drumming with a single child's voice singing to the tune of 'The Maple Leaf Forever."

Our story holds a painful truth.
Many hearts still tender be.
We honour those we lost too soon,
And all who carry the legacy.
Let's laugh and cry and learn to be
Joined in truth together
To move beyond the need to sing
"The Maple Leaf Forever."[1]

Lights up on a classroom in a fictional Anglican Residential School in northern Ontario in late January 1939. It is evening.

JEAN DELORME and FATHER WILLIAMS enter.

WILLIAMS: Where's Joseph? I thought you'd both be done by 7:00 pm sharp?

JEAN: He was still in the barn when I finished my chores, Father.

---

[1] "The Maple Leaf Forever," words and music by Alexander Muir, composed in 1867.

WILLIAMS: Just because MacFarlane runs the farm doesn't mean he can ignore direct orders from Principal Clarke. Stay here and tell the girls where I've gone.

JEAN: Yes, Coach... the girls?

> *FATHER WILLIAMS looks back at JEAN and then exits. A moment later BETH SUMMERS enters.*

BETH: What are you doing on the girls' side of the school?

> *She begins erasing the chalkboard.*

JEAN: I'm meeting with Father Williams to... to discuss strategy for Saturday's hockey game. I think. Look, what's your name?

BETH: I could get into trouble for even speaking to you.

JEAN: Or for breathing. Or for standing up too straight. Or for looking out the window. So, you might as well tell me your name.

BETH: Everyone knows you can't trust a half-breed.

JEAN: Doesn't make the strap feel any softer.

> *JOSEPH SUMMERS runs in, out of breath. He stops in his tracks at the sight of his sister BETH and soon scurries over to JEAN as MISS AP DAFYDD (Pronounced "Sharn Ap Davith"), FATHER WILLIAMS, EVELYNE RICE, and SUSAN BLACKBIRD enter.*

AP DAFYDD: Where are the others? I thought you were bringing eight boys in total? *(Turning to the chalkboard.)* Beth, the board!

BETH finishes cleaning the chalkboard.

WILLIAMS: How was I to know that most of the boys can barely read English, let alone Shakespeare?

AP DAFYDD: Shakespeare is English.

WILLIAMS: Have a seat, Summers.

Both JOSEPH and BETH go to sit at this instruction.

AP DAFYDD: Two Summers? What a coincidence.

BETH: *(A little too quickly.)*   JOSEPH: *(With BETH.)* It's quite a common   Lots of Summers up name up north.   north.

AP DAFYDD: Well, it's certainly easier to pronounce than some of those complicated names you have. You can call me Miss Ap Dafydd. *(She writes "Miss Ap Dafydd" on the chalkboard.)* Father Williams, this is Beth Summers, Evelyne Rice, and Susan Blackbird; no doubt they'd remember you from your services.

BETH/
EVELYNE/
SUSAN: *(They curtsy.)* Good evening, Father Williams.

WILLIAMS: Good evening, girls.

AP DAFYDD: *(To JEAN.)* And which one are you?

JEAN: #119.

WILLIAMS: She means your name.

JEAN: Sorry, Coach. Jean Delorme, Miss Ap Daf—I mean, Ma'am.

WILLIAMS: *(To JEAN.)* You're going to have to learn how to speak properly in front of the King.

SUSAN: The King?

BETH: Like, the *King* King?

EVELYNE: From the picture in the mess hall?

AP DAFYDD: Indeed!

JEAN: *(To FATHER WILLIAMS.)* The King likes hockey?

AP DAFYDD: Dear boy, this is about something far more important than hockey.

JEAN: Football?!

JOSEPH: Are we being punished for something?

AP DAFYDD: On the contrary, you've been hand-picked as our brightest students. *(She pulls out a newspaper and reads.)* "The announcement that Their Majesties King George VI and Queen Elizabeth have graciously decided to visit Canada in the months of May and June has been received with rejoicing throughout the Dominion."

WILLIAMS: *(Taking the paper.)* "The honour of welcoming their King and Queen, in person, on their own soil, is a privilege, which will be shared with enthusiasm and pride by all His Majesty's Canadian subjects."

AP DAFYDD: And, we've been informed that their Majesties are interested in visiting our school to witness firsthand how well you're learning to be good little Canadians. And to prove that, I am going to—

WILLIAMS: *(Jumping in.)* We're treating them to a play.

AP DAFYDD: *(Jumping back in.)* Directed by me!

WILLIAMS: And I've been appointed the school's official liaison to the royal reception on behalf of the Women's Auxiliary.

AP DAFYDD: "The webbe of our life, is of a mingled yarne, good and ill together: our vertues would bee proud, if our faults whipt them not, and our crimes would dispaire if they were not cherish'd by our vertues."

> *BETH and JEAN raise their hands emphatically. MISS AP DAFYDD nods to JEAN.*

JEAN: Is that Louis Riel?

WILLIAMS: Delorme, that's Our Lord and Saviour, Jesus Christ.

AP DAFYDD: *(Flustered, turning to the students.)* No, no, it's Shakespeare. It's William Shakespeare.

BETH: *(Aside, to JEAN.)* I knew it.

AP DAFYDD: The perfect offering for their Majesties!

WILLIAMS: He's no Gilbert and Sullivan...

AP DAFYDD: I'll venture none of you have ever heard of Shakespeare until you came to this school.

> *JEAN barely raises his hand. MISS AP DAFYDD nods.*

JEAN: My apologies, Miss Ap Daffy, I mean Ap Dafydd, I never heard of him till tonight.

> *JOSEPH nods.*

AP DAFYDD: Tonight? Father Williams, is Principal Clarke aware of this?

WILLIAMS: He's the one who approved Shakespeare's... *It All Turns Out Well in the End.*

BETH: Do you mean *All's Well That End Well?* That's a marvellous play!

JOSEPH: *(Aside.)* Sounds like a waste of time.

JEAN: *(Aside, to JOSEPH.)* Sounds like a dream I had once.

AP DAFYDD: The play depicts Helena, a virtuous young woman, who delivers a miracle by saving the King's life. He grants her whatever she desires and with that she chooses to marry her secret love, the young soldier Bertram. But "The course of true love never did run smooth."

BETH/
AP DAFYDD: *A Midsummer Night's Dream;* Act 1, Scene 1

AP DAFYDD: Bertram proves to be a callous young man, not able yet to accept the gift of a good wife. But Helena is cunning and, eventually... all's well that ends well.

SUSAN: Any witches in this one?

AP DAFYDD: I left some bits out: there's a Countess and a clown, and some other soldiers, and so on, no witches, but Helena's ingenuity —

WILLIAMS: And her faith...

AP DAFYDD: And her faith, are at the heart of this story, which is why it's a perfect fit for our monarchs.

WILLIAMS: Not to mention that they win a war! The Commonwealth must do its part in what may come.

EVELYNE: Do we get costumes?

AP DAFYDD: Of course!

JEAN:	Will there be singing and dancing?
AP DAFYDD:	That will not be necessary.
BETH:	When do we find out which roles we're playing?
AP DAFYDD:	Ideally, next week. But the royal visit to our school has yet to be announced, so we've all got to keep this a secret until the cat's out of the bag.
WILLIAMS:	With the royal visit, the "Who's Who" of northern Ontario will finally understand how worthy this institution is of their financial support. We'll have the Almighty to thank if the roof makes it through the winter.
AP DAFYDD:	We'll all be working together over the course of the next several months—
WILLIAMS:	Every Thursday, at 7 pm sharp.
JOSEPH:	We're short-handed on the farm since Logan ran—disappeared.
JEAN:	Last week a cow got frostbit on one of her teats; Joe had to spend the whole night blowing on it.
SUSAN:	That's a lot of hot air.
AP DAFYDD:	Susan! First and foremost, this is a school, farm duties must take a back seat to learning.
WILLIAMS:	Well, at certain times of the year.
JOSEPH:	(To FATHER WILLIAMS.) I was told, after I graduated, that the only thing I had to do to get home was work on the farm.
	Silence, as the students assess the reaction of the adults.

WILLIAMS: There's a lot of boys who'd be desperate to be in your shoes, Summers.

JOSEPH: My shoes aren't worth anyone's desperation.

WILLIAMS: Joseph Summers, on top of your farm duties, you now have extra dish duty for a week.

AP DAFYDD: And not to worry, you'll all look fabulous in tights!

> *JOSEPH and JEAN look at each other in horror.*

Transition 1.1-1.2

> *SUSAN animates one of the chalkboards with the words "Home?" and "Cree?"*
>
> *MISS AP DAFYDD erases it.*

Scene 1.2

> *JOSEPH is in the kitchen doing dishes — the last remaining clean-up after a special meeting of the staff and distinguished guests at the school discussing the prospect of the play.*
>
> *BETH arrives with a tray of fine china tea cups and a plate with three leftover biscuits.*

BETH: "How much better it is to weepe at joy, than to joy—"

> *JOSEPH, startled, abruptly stops and turns to see BETH munching on one of the biscuits.*

JOSEPH: Jesus, Beth! Keep your voice down! What if someone walked in here right now?

BETH: It was Miss Ap Dafydd who asked me to clean up. It's not our fault we're both here at the same time.

JOSEPH: But I'll be the one that gets the brunt of it. Remember when Father Becker caught us talking in the schoolyard?

BETH: May he rest in peace.

JOSEPH: Put me in the hellhole under the stairs for three days.

BETH: I'm sorry, Joe.

JOSEPH: You'd better go.

BETH turns to leave, dejected, when JOSEPH stops her.

Wait. Ni-minjinawez. *(I'm sorry).*

She stops and turns to JOSEPH.

BETH: Don't you miss me?

JOSEPH: What happens when they remember that you're my little sister?

BETH: You're one of the only boys who can actually read. I think you'll like Shakespeare. The boys get to play with swords *and* there are a lot of fart jokes.

JOSEPH: I don't trust them, Beth.

BETH: I just watched Miss Ap Dafydd fight for us in front of some mean-looking men from town who don't think that we can do Shakespeare like it should be done. She told them we would make them proud.

JOSEPH: I don't want to make *them* proud, I want it to be better for us.

He reaches for her hand but is interrupted by the sound of a door opening and closing. They freeze until the coast is clear. JOSEPH resumes his task.

They change the rules whenever they want. I thought I was outta here last year after I graduated and now, I have to work until I can pay for the bush plane. They've kept some boys on the farm for years. I just want to go home, Beth. I want us both to go home to our family.

BETH: Even though there hasn't been one word from them in seven years?

JOSEPH: We don't know that. So many parents get turned away at the gate.

BETH: Then why not a letter!

JOSEPH: You know Principal Clarke reads everything... If our parents mention the twins, they'll end up here too.

BETH: Well, Shakespeare's words make me feel alive. I just want to feel alive.

Silence.

JOSEPH: All right, but no tights. I won't wear tights.

BETH pockets one of the remaining biscuits. JOSEPH grins and watches her go before returning to his task.

Transition 1.2-1.3

> *JEAN animates one of the chalkboards with the beginning of a letter to his mother: "Dear Mama, I'm in a play."*
>
> *FATHER WILLIAMS erases it.*

Scene 1.3

> *First rehearsal, girls' classroom. All are gathered.*

AP DAFYDD: Father Williams, were you not successful in your mission?

WILLIAMS: Sergeant Berhn wouldn't let me pull any boys from the marching band.

AP DAFYDD: Let's put a notice up at the church in town, in hopes that some enthusiastic parishioners would be interested in some of the minor roles.

SUSAN: That'd be a major surprise.

AP DAFYDD: Susan! I've made special arrangements to borrow the only copy of *The Complete Works of Shakespeare* from the library in town, *(Indicates the one FATHER WILLIAMS is holding.)* which means there will be consequences if even a page is ruffled. Beth, you're in charge.

> *FATHER WILLIAMS almost drops the book as he passes it to BETH.*

Father Williams and I will use my personal copy.

BETH: So... is today when we find out what roles we're playing, Miss Ap Dafydd?

JEAN:	Would it be possible to make a request?
AP DAFYDD:	I'm surprised you'd want to.
JEAN:	I had a chance to look through the play during hockey practice.
WILLIAMS:	*(To MISS AP DAFYDD.)* I had just come from the library.
JEAN:	I skimmed it while Billy was using the skates we share; it seems obvious who I should play.
AP DAFYDD:	*Whom* you should play.
JEAN:	Whom? The Métis one, *Pay*-roles.
AP DAFYDD:	It's pronounced Pa-*roll*-eez —
WILLIAMS:	There's a half-breed in this play? I don't know if Principal Clarke / would approve.
AP DAFYDD:	Of course there isn't!
JEAN:	My apologies ApDaff... I mean Mrs., I mean Miss Ap Daffy-dd.
AP DAFYDD:	If it means that much to you, you may play Parolles.
JEAN:	Thank you, ma'am. I mean, Miss!
AP DAFYDD:	Now, Joseph, that leaves Bertram to you.
JOSEPH:	The "callous" one?
AP DAFYDD:	He's the son of the Countess, he's a young nobleman.
BETH:	He may be callous, but he's also very brave.
EVELYNE:	Like you.

JOSEPH blushes.

BETH:	Bertram is the reluctant hero, Joe— seph.

AP DAFYDD:	Quite right Beth, I see you've been studying up too. Sounds like something the Countess would do.
BETH:	The Countess?
AP DAFYDD:	Yes, and Evelyne will be playing Helena and Susan will play Diana.
SUSAN:	I *am* a straight-shooter.

MISS AP DAFYDD laughs at SUSAN's joke.

BETH:	But I'm the youngest of the group, I thought I'd be playing... someone more my age.
AP DAFYDD:	Beth, your maturity and intelligence lend themselves perfectly to this role.
JOSEPH:	You'll be great, Beth.
WILLIAMS:	It's all well and good for an Indian to play a Countess, but we can't have one playing the King. Our royal guests would be horrified.
AP DAFYDD:	But it's the King of France in this play. Now, a special treat from my personal collection. Beth, set us up, please.

BETH uncovers a gramophone, carefully dropping the needle on the record.

Dame Ellen Terry, our generation's finest Shakespearean actress, as Juliet, in 1911.

MISS AP DAFYDD mouths every word.

RECORDING:	*"Come Viall, what if this mixture do not worke at all?* *Shall I be married then tomorrow morning?* *No, no, this shall forbid it. Lie thou there.* *What if it be a poison which the Friar* *Subtly hath ministered to have me dead—*

> *to have me dead —*
> *to have me dead — "*

> *The record begins to skip from overuse.*
> *BETH lifts the needle. The other students*
> *look at each other in horror.*

JOSEPH: *(Aside, to EVELYNE.) We're* supposed to do that?

AP DAFYDD: We must all aspire to Terry's example of how it should be done! Now the play begins with a goodbye to Bertram, who is off to live as a ward of the King of France, who is deathly ill with a fistula.

WILLIAMS: Oh, Brother Dean had a fistula last autumn, it was disgusting!

AP DAFYDD: Let's have a look at the Countess's farewell speech to her son Bertram. Beth, you get us started, page 293 in your book. Everyone, pay close attention to Beth's command of the language. *(Indicating that BETH should begin.)* And!

BETH: *(British accent but monotone, still miffed about her casting.)*
Be thou blest Bertrame and succeed thy father
In manners as in shape —

AP DAFYDD: Beth, remember what Dame Ellen Terry said, "To act, you must make the thing written your own."[2] Try to remember when Alice was sent to the sanatorium, you cried for a week.

JOSEPH: *(Aside, to EVELYNE.)* Why do we have to do Shakespeare with British accents?

---

[2] From *The Story of My Life* by Ellen Terry, first published by Hutchinson & Co, London, 1900.

EVELYNE: *(Aside, to JOSEPH)* Miss Ap Dafydd says it doesn't make sense otherwise.

BETH: *(Turns her anger into long vowels, more in line with Ellen Terry's recording.)*
Be thou blest Bertrame and succeed thy father
In manners as in shape: thy blood and vertue Contend for Empire in thee, and thy goodnesse
Share with thy birth-right.

AP DAFYDD: Better! So, the Countess is urging her son to be guided by his nobility as he ventures out into the world without his loving parent for the first time. What other advice does she offer, Joseph?

> *BETH hands* The Complete Works *to JOSEPH, pointing to where he should continue reading.*

JOSEPH: *(Without an accent.)*
"Love all, trust a few…"
That's pretty good advice.

AP DAFYDD: Just read the text. With the accent.

JOSEPH: *(High register voice, imitating Terry.)*
Doe wrong to none—

AP DAFYDD: No, in your own voice.

JOSEPH: *(In his own voice, no accent.)* …be able for thine enemy—

AP DAFYDD: No, not *your* voice, like Dame Ellen Terry does it, just… lower.

JOSEPH: *(Whispering, with the accent.)* Rather in power then use: and keepe thy friend
Under thy owne lifes key.

AP DAFYDD: Next time, you'll have to try using your outside voice.

JEAN: Like when you're calling the pigs back into the pen.

SUSAN: Ham it up.

> *FATHER WILLIAMS guffaws; he's the only one who finds it funny.*

AP DAFYDD: Susan, not the advice Shakespeare's actors would have received, but apt enough. Father Williams, you'll have to work on the dialect with your boys before our next rehearsal.

WILLIAMS: You mean—

AP DAFYDD: Did your grandmother not grow up in England?

WILLIAMS: Well yes, but—

AP DAFYDD: Just teach the boys to speak exactly as she did.

Transition 1.3-1.4

> *JOSEPH animates one of the chalkboards with Anishinaabemowin: "Gaakaabishiikwe" (Hawk woman).*

> *FATHER WILLIAMS erases it.*

Scene 1.4

> *BETH, followed by SUSAN and EVELYNE, enters the girls' bathroom. It's 3 am. BETH is wearing her wool blanket, tied around her waist to indicate a long skirt. The other two are holding theirs.*

EVELYNE: *(Whispering.)* Why here, Beth? You know what happens in this bathroom.

SUSAN: This place gives me the creeps.

EVELYNE: What were you thinking? This is risky—

BETH: Miss Ap Dafydd is relying on *me* to make sure *you*... Just take your blankets and tie them around your waist.

BETH assists the other two.

EVELYNE: Why are you so keen on Ap Daffy anyway?

SUSAN: Yeah, even the other teachers seem to hate her.

BETH: She is trying to teach us how to be good actresses, like Ellen Terry!

SUSAN: So I can perform a Shakespeare monologue to the sheets I'm scrubbing?

BETH: No, so that you can do more than scrub sheets forever.

EVELYNE: And to do that we need to walk like the boys in the marching band?

SUSAN: At least these blankets are finally useful for something.

As BETH straightens SUSAN's back she gasps and pulls away.

BETH: Again?

SUSAN: Am I bleeding?

EVELYNE: No.

Beat.

SUSAN: Let's get on with it.

BETH: "Eyes right! Chest out! Chin tucked in!"

BETH recites as she walks, lightly kicking the blanket out from under her feet so as not to trip.

In his bright radiance and colaterall light;
Th' ambition in my love thus plagues it selfe:
The hind that would be mated by the Lion
Must die for love.

EVELYNE and SUSAN join in, but their light kicks quickly evolve into "kicking at the blanket and progressing in jumps like young kangaroos."[3]

EVELYNE/
SUSAN: The hind that would be mated by the Lion
Must die for love.

EVELYNE trips on the blanket and falls. SUSAN and EVELYNE let out a muffled squeal.

EVELYNE: So, Helena is a hind, as in a deer?

SUSAN: Yeah, and Joe's the lion.

SUSAN roars at EVELYNE, clawing the air. They descend into giggles.

BETH: Joe's more like a moose. He's stubborn.

EVELYNE: Takes courage to stand up for what you believe in.

BETH: "Follow the rules and you will survive," that's what the older girls told me when I first got here.

EVELYNE: You're breaking the rules even bringing us here.

---

[3] From *The Story of My Life* bby Ellen Terry, first published by Hutchinson & Co, London, 1900.

BETH:	"Work hard and you will be rewarded; Follow Jesus and you will be loved."
SUSAN:	Still waiting on that love.
BETH:	Well, I'm just looking for some hope.
EVELYNE:	In the white man's world?

The three girls freeze as they hear footsteps approaching.

SUSAN:	Let's all be deer and bound out of here.

The girls disappear into the darkness as the sound of footsteps gets closer.

Transition 1.4-1.5

*MISS AP DAFYDD writes a line of iambic pentameter on the central chalkboard marking the stressed and unstressed syllables: "His **arched brows**, his **hawking** eyes, his **curls**."*

Scene 1.5

Midway through the second rehearsal. The students and FATHER WILLIAMS are cantering like horses, in the Ellen Terry style, repeating lines back at MISS AP DAFYDD.

ALL:	Of every line and tricke of his / sweet favour.
AP DAFYDD:	All right, let's try this section again *(Under her breath.)* for the fifth time. Like horses, clip-clop actors! *(Pointing to the board.)* His arched browes, his hawking eye, his curles—
ALL:	His arched browes, his hawking eye, his curles—

AP DAFYDD: I don't understand why you're not getting this; don't you all ride horses?

> *JEAN raises his hand, MISS AP DAFYDD nods.*

JEAN: Did people actually talk in iambic pentameter back then?

AP DAFYDD: Only the poets, Jean.

EVELYNE: Like our storytellers, when they use music and—

AP DAFYDD: Evelyne, what have I told you?

EVELYNE: That I have to forget all of that... "nonsense."

> *MISS AP DAFYDD starts the exercise again.*

AP DAFYDD: In our hearts table: heart too capeable.

ALL: *(Starting to fall apart.)*
In our hearts table: (f)heart too capeable
Of every line and tricke of his sweet favour.

> *JEAN and BETH are doing their best, SUSAN stubs a toe, EVELYNE whinnies, everyone rolls their "R"s, and JOSEPH deliberately trips JEAN.*

AP DAFYDD: Stop, stop stop! *(Taking a deep breath.)* Let's call it a day.

WILLIAMS: Tomorrow we'll gather for you to write out your lines so that memorization can begin. You're dismissed.

> *They leave quickly, sensing MISS AP DAFYDD's frustration. FATHER WILLIAMS continues to practise the exercise.*

"I would I had that corporall soundnesse now."

AP DAFYDD: Father Williams, please be careful with that book, it was my father's prized possession.

WILLIAMS: *(Carefully handing the book back.)* This technique could really transform my sermons.

AP DAFYDD: This is a travesty; Mr. Martin has utterly failed these boys. My girls were even infected with their ineptitude. Shakespeare should be a fundamental in English class no matter who the student is.

WILLIAMS: Can't hit the back of the net the first time you shoot a puck.

AP DAFYDD: There are no pucks in Shakespeare.

WILLIAMS: Miss Ap... May I call you Sian? *(Pronouncing it phonetically.)*

AP DAFYDD: It's pronounced "Sharn."

WILLIAMS: Shane, Principal Clarke is relying on us to impress the King so that we can attract substantial donations to the school, this roof won't—

AP DAFYDD: Yes, I know about the roof.

WILLIAMS: This is no time to be discouraged, took me three attempts to be ordained, but look at me now! Isn't it always like this at the beginning of the season?

> *Smacking her back, the book goes flying, the two watch in horror as it lands with a thud.*

Transition 1.5-1.6

> *MISS AP DAFYDD erases. the line of iambic pentameter on the central chalkboard.*

Scene 1.6

> *Students are each sitting at a desk writing out or studying their lines. JEAN has one book and is quietly sounding out the pronunciation of the word "egregious" throughout the scene. BETH has the other book. SUSAN and EVELYNE are memorizing their lines. FATHER WILLIAMS sits in the corner, reading the sports section of the paper. We hear JOSEPH's inner thoughts.*

JOSEPH: *(Trying to remember his mother's song.)* Gi-maamin... Gi-maaminonen... Gi-maaminonenimaa. *(He sings the beginning, triumphantly.)* Gi-maaminonenimaa na gi-maamaa e-gigiinoo'amaag ozaawegizigewin. We'd sit by the river and you'd sing to us ni maamaa, Beth would braid my hair... Do you think it'll take long to grow again? *(He looks to BETH.)* Gaakaabishiikwe *(Hawk woman)*, do you remember the songs ni-maamaanaan would sing? Her voice was so beautiful. You sing like her, *(Chucking regretfully.)* I sound like mbaabaa *(Papa)*. I guess I'd be too old to sit with the women. I'll be going out with the hunters, if I ever get home. Do you remember our last winter up north, the Indian agent only let four hunters leave the reserve?

> *BETH walks the book over to SUSAN and returns to her desk.*

The party returned with only two caribou; not enough meat for the winter, but you were so happy you sang ni-maamaanaan's favourite song and told everyone that next year, you were going to kill three caribou! Mmmm, caribou. And deer... waawaashkeshi-wag, and rabbit stew... waabooz niboop! Can't wait to eat good meat again. I want to be a hunter, not a farmer! Though maybe it wouldn't be so bad if I actually got eat the crops I grew. What if I've forgotten how to hunt? Mbaabaa *(Papa)* will remind me, he was always so patient. I'll help him provide for the family. I can teach the twins where to pick the best berries! Remember Gaakaabishiikwe *(Hawk woman)*, when the berries were finally sweet, we'd stuff ourselves. Well, no, you always filled your apron for the old ones first, while the *rest* of us stuffed ourselves. You were always thinking of others. You had a spark in your eye, like the stars. We'd sit at the river late at night and you would name the constellations. Gi-gii-wiinge-Jiikendam, gi-gii-niim gaye gi-gii-biibaag wiinzowinan iwedi giizhigong; Maang-Anangoog, Ojiig-Anangoog, Madoodoswaan-Anangoog *(You got so excited, you danced and shouted the names to the sky; Little Dipper, Big Dipper, Corona Borealis.)* Is that little girl gone forever, Beth?

JEAN: "Egregious"!

WILLIAMS: Shhh!

Scene 1.7

One week later (third rehearsal). Everyone, except for JOSEPH, is assembled. The students have their notebooks with their dialogue and cues written out. BETH is

> *helping the other girls tie their blankets around their waists. FATHER WILLIAMS and MISS AP DAFYDD are in a private conversation.*

AP DAFYDD: If we were the Titsworth Academy, it wouldn't be an issue.

WILLIAMS: Several members of the Women's Auxiliary signed up, but their husbands crossed them off again. *(To the students.)* Listen up, everyone, there won't be any new recruits, so our first line will be doing double duty. That reminds me, good hustle on Saturday, Delorme. We've got a real shot at making the finals.

AP DAFYDD: All right, the end of Act I, Scene 1, Helena and Parolles. How's your dialect coming, Jean?

JEAN: *(With a thick Cockney accent.)* Fine and dandy, Miss Ap Dafydd!

AP DAFYDD: Father Williams, what have you done?

WILLIAMS: Taught them to speak exactly as my nan did.

AP DAFYDD: You should have told me.

JEAN: *(Looking pleadingly to FATHER WILLIAMS.)* It's how I learned it!

AP DAFYDD: I'll fix it later.

> *EVELYNE and JEAN stand up with their notebooks.*

Now... this is the meeting of Helena and Bertram's seemingly loyal friend, Parolles. And!

EVELYNE: *(As Helena, in the Ellen Terry style throughout.)* Who comes here?

JEAN: *(As Parolles, with a Cockney accent throughout.)* I enter.

AP DAFYDD: That's a stage direction ,Jean, just do it.

JEAN: Sorry, Miss ApDaff... ididi...

(As Parolles.)
Save you faire Queene.

EVELYNE: *(As Helena.)*
And you Monarch.

JEAN: *(As Parolles.)*
Are you meditating on *(Pause.)* virginitie?

WILLIAMS: Delorme, let me see that.

AP DAFYDD: Father Williams, this is the whole point of the scene, Parolles is encouraging Helena to marry.

SUSAN: Like Principal Clarke with Lucas Wenjack and me; he's encouraging us to marry by telling us we have to.

WILLIAMS: Miss Ap Dafydd! Is this truly an appropriate subject to be addressing in front of our King?

AP DAFYDD: No doubt the King would appreciate a virtuous girl who defends her virginity using wit and ingenuity. Carry on, Evelyne.

EVELYNE: *(As Helena.)*
I will stand for't a little, though therefore I die a Virgin.

JOSEPH enters to hear "die a virgin," EVELYNE is thoroughly embarrassed.

JOSEPH: Sorry I'm late, the chickens are moulting; they're miserable.

He takes off his cap and feathers fly out.

AP DAFYDD: Well, they aren't the only ones. Where were we?

JEAN: I was talking about virgins.

WILLIAMS: Delorme!

JEAN: Sorry, Coach.

AP DAFYDD: And!

JEAN: *(As Parolles.)*
Virginitie breeds mites, much like a Cheese, besides Virginitie is peevish, proud, idle, made of self-love. Keepe it not, you cannot choose but loose by't.

EVELYNE: *(As Helena.)*
How might one do sir, to lose it to her owne liking?

JEAN: *(As Parolles.)*
'Tis a commodity will lose the gloss with lying: For your virginity, your old virginity— it looks ill, it eates drily, marry 'tis a wither'd peare—

WILLIAMS: A withered pear!? Not another word out of you, Delorme.

JEAN: Shakespeare's the perverted one, not me!

WILLIAMS: A moment, Miss Ap Dafydd.

AP DAFYDD: Very well. Beth, you're in charge. I suggest everyone start learning your lines.

    The teachers hover in the doorway. The students, except for BETH, crack up in disbelief.

JEAN: "Virginitie breeds mites, much like a Cheese."

BETH: Grow up! We need to be taking this seriously.

EVELYNE:	Acting is so confusing.
JEAN:	*(To EVELYNE.)* You're more like Helena than you think.
BETH:	Oh, and why would that be?
JEAN:	Evelyne clearly comes from a family of medicine people.
JOSEPH:	Is that true?
JEAN:	I've seen you in the back field tending to burns and lashes, putting on herbs—
EVELYNE:	Medicines.
JEAN:	Medicines. My mama used to talk about how the old people would use them on her reserve.
JOSEPH:	That takes a lot of courage, doing that under their noses.
JEAN:	I tried to do it myself once, after MacFarlane nailed me in the head, but I got this weird scar. *(He feels the scar.)* Wanna feel it?
BETH/ EVELYNE/ SUSAN:	No!
SUSAN:	Shhh, here they come.
	FATHER WILLIAMS and MISS AP DAFYDD re-enter.
AP DAFYDD:	I am pleased to announce that the scene will remain *and* Father Williams has graciously accepted to play the role of the King.
	She applauds and encourages the students to join her.

WILLIAMS: Of course, I don't take this role on lightly, particularly considering that I will be giving my King of France, before the King of England; whom, we all know, were historic rivals.

AP DAFYDD: *Who* we all know... never mind.

    The evening bell rings.

Transition 1.7-1.8

    BETH animates a chalkboard with practising her cursive writing: "Th'ambition in my love thus plagues itself."

Scene 1.8

    With little light except the twinkle of stars and a wisp of a moon, we see EVELYNE perched (sitting) on the slanted roof. It is cold. She tries to calm her shaking body.

EVELYNE: *(Looking up at the stars.)* Raksótha *(Grampa)*, I want to go home. Can you show me the way? Send me a sign? If I got down from this roof and ran away now, this very moment, would I make it? Rake'níha enhanà:khwen'ne toka' kanónhskon ièn:ke... *(Dad wouldn't be happy, me showing up...)* his new white wife and all... she even wears Mom's favourite apron... Nek tsi kwah tsi niiohsera'taksèn:'ne ki tsohséra tsi nahé *(but this has been the worst year of my life).*

EVELYNE: *(As Helena.)* "Our remedies oft in ourselves do lye,
Which we ascribe to heaven: the fated skye
Gives us free scope..."

She stops and breathes deeply, feeling freedom for the first time in a long time.

Remember that night we fell asleep looking at the stars, Grampa? We were so sore the next day. *(As her Grampa.)* "Hà:ke Onkwehónwehneha nitia'tó:ten? Konia'tí:saks ne akwanaktí:io." *("What kind of Indian am I? Miss my soft bed!")*

"Miss my soft bed!". We laughed so hard. "Iotsistohkwarón:nion tehshonkwa'-shatstenhserá:wis" *("Stars show us the way and give us strength").*

A Northern Saw-whet Owl calls in the night. EVELYNE freezes.

Shh! You want me to get caught?

The owl hoots again.

I won't hurt you. You and me, we're the same. They took our land away from us too. Can you swoop me up and bring me home to Kahnawá:ke?

She watches the owl fly away.

Yeah, didn't think so.

EVELYNE: *(As Helena.)*
"...the fated skye
Gives us free scope, only doth backward pull
Our slow designes, when we ourselves are dull."

Well I'm not dull! Kwah tsi wa'kate'nièn:ten ne akaté:ko! *(I tried everything).* Came here kicking and screaming. You would have stood up for me Grampa, if you were still alive. I know it. I can still feel you standing beside me, though. Nowèn:ton tsi nikahá:wi enthonhenréhte tsi ónen'k tsi enke'nikónhrhen *(No matter how much they tell me I should)*, I don't want to forget how you gently talked to each plant before you picked it for medicine or the way you laughed. *(Giggles.)* Joseph laughs like you did... You would like Helena, she reminds me of Mom. Iah te eniakoteríhshon *(She refuses to give up)*. She refuses to give up.

> *EVELYNE makes a connection.*

"To act, you must make the thing written your own."

> *She leaps up in excitement and exits.*

Transition 1.8-1.9

> *A spirit image appears on one of the chalkboards.*

> *JOSEPH erases BETH's line of cursive text: "Th'ambition in my love thus plagues itself."*

Scene 1.9

> *In the visitation room, FATHER WILLIAMS and MISS AP DAFYDD are concluding an interview with a reporter in her early 60s named MADGE MACBETH. EVELYNE stands nearby, next to the remnants of a tea service, which she was tasked to serve. MRS. MACBETH is writing in her notepad.*

MACBETH: Very good, very good... an excellent perspective, Miss Ap Dafydd.

WILLIAMS: You said your train was at two?

                MRS. MACBETH looks at her watch.

MACBETH: Indeed, I must take my leave of you.

                MRS. MACBETH starts packing up her things. FATHER WILLIAMS offers her coat as she turns to EVELYNE.

                Are you in the play, young lady?

                EVELYNE nods.

AP DAFYDD: Evelyne's playing Helena.

MACBETH: And what do you make of Shakespeare, Evelyne?

WILLIAMS: I don't think your readers would be much interested in—

AP DAFYDD: Mrs. Macbeth has written articles in the *Canadian Courier* and *Mayfair* magazines! Clearly, she wants to hear from Evelyne.

WILLIAMS: Whose task it was to serve tea.

MACBETH: And who's an integral part of your production.

                MRS. MACBETH guides EVELYNE to sit. EVELYNE looks to MISS AP DAFYDD who nods encouragingly. As EVELYNE sits, MRS. MACBETH pours her a cup of tea.

EVELYNE: Miss Ap Dafydd says that Shakespeare mirrors life, that his characters are real people, like us.

MACBETH: *(To MISS AP DAFYDD.)* If only we had such enlightened directors at the Ottawa Drama League.

EVELYNE: I think my grampa would have liked him.

AP DAFYDD: Evelyne...

WILLIAMS: That's enough. One can hardly expect the students to express themselves articulately in an important interview such as this.

MACBETH: Not to worry, that's what editors are for. Evelyne, what do you hope the King and Queen will take from your production?

EVELYNE: That they see us for who we really are.

> *MRS. MACBETH writes down EVELYNE's words.*

WILLIAMS: Only the eyes of God can truly see, Evelyne. Now Miss Mac—

MACBETH: It's Mrs. actually. My / husband...

WILLIAMS: Ah, I see, you are married—

MACBETH: My husband / was...

WILLIAMS: Named Macbeth, such a conundrum. He must be—

AP DAFYDD: Father Williams, if you don't mind.

WILLIAMS: It's just that you rarely hear of journalists who are... well... women.

MACBETH: I'm more than just a journalist, I write everything but hymns.[4]

WILLIAMS: Your husband must be—

---

[4] *Ottawa Citizen*, 23 March, 1964

MACBETH: Dead, Father Williams. I lost both my husband and my father to tuberculosis. Terrible disease. It's taken many of your students, has it not?

                EVELYNE rattles the tea cup; MISS AP DAFYDD and FATHER WILLIAMS give her a stern look; MRS. MACBETH looks at her watch.

                Oh, I'm going to miss my train.

                FATHER WILLIAMS helps her with her coat.

WILLIAMS: Well, in my capacity as the school's official liaison to the royal reception on behalf of the Women's Auxiliary, I am most pleased that the *Ottawa Citizen* has shown an interest in our school's production!

MACBETH: It's certainly one of the more unique offerings on Their Majesties' agenda. I admire your efforts to offer the Indians an opportunity to appreciate the glories of fine literature.

WILLIAMS: Now that's an excellent quote for your article.

MACBETH: In general, I prefer not to quote myself.

AP DAFYDD: I cannot express how inspiring it's been to meet you... a real privilege...

MACBETH: I hope I can highlight your innovative production.

WILLIAMS: *(Shaking her hand.)* How did you find out about our little endeavour in the first place?

MACBETH: You know, Father Williams, politicians speak to their wives *(Crosses to MISS AP DAFYDD and shakes her hand.)* and women speak to each other. Good day to you all.

> *MRS. MACBETH begins to exit; MISS AP DAFYDD and FATHER WILLIAMS follow her out.*

AP DAFYDD: You must be able to relate to the students doing Shakespeare because of your own acting experience.

WILLIAMS: Can you imagine, dressing up as Hiawatha and performing for tourists?

AP DAFYDD: Not to mention interviewing debutantes and diplomats!

> *EVELYNE, left alone, grabs the remaining tea biscuits before exiting.*

Transition 1.9-1.10

> *BETH animates one of the chalkboards, practising her cursive writing: "They, that they cannot help."*
>
> *JOSEPH erases it.*

Scene 1.10

> *Classroom. One bucket is in the corner collecting water from the leaking roof. STUDENTS, still carrying their notebooks, are mid-conversation; the girls have their blankets tied around their waists. MISS AP DAFYDD and FATHER WILLIAMS are not present.*

BETH: Just because Helena knows medicines doesn't make her Indian.

EVELYNE: She also has faith in the stars. People don't believe in her, but she knows women are strong, medicines are powerful.

JOSEPH: Helena has been "adopted" and "educated" by the "nice" white lady.

JEAN: And they won't let her cry about her dead father. Even the youngest ones here get punished for that.

BETH: She doesn't even remember her father.

SUSAN: They keep reminding us that forgetting is the most important lesson to remember.

BETH: You're all completely missing the point; this is Shakespeare.

JEAN: The play does end with Helena winning Bertram over. We'd be showing an Indian girl marrying a rich white guy! Like my mama. Except for the rich part. Oh, and I guess she'd lose her Indian status if she married a white guy, like my mama. But ya know, at least she'd be rich. Not like my mama.

BETH: It's not how Shakespeare is supposed to be done!

Enter MISS AP DAFYDD, flustered. They all stop immediately.

AP DAFYDD: *(Looking around.)* Where is Father Williams?

JOSEPH: We just saw him pacing in the hallway; he's trying to learn his lines, I think.

AP DAFYDD: Let's begin, Act I, Scene 3, the Countess has discovered that Helena loves her son, Bertram, and learns of Helena's plan to go to Paris to try to cure the King's disease. Jean, you're on book. *(No one gets their notebooks out.)* Is there a problem?

EVELYNE: *(Cautiously.)* Miss Ap Dafydd, I have an idea.

AP DAFYDD: Well, I'm curious to hear ideas.

EVELYNE: I thought that maybe... I think Helena... could possibly be a Mohawk girl, like me.

AP DAFYDD: I beg your pardon?

EVELYNE: Helena's trying to find her way in the white man's world, just like us, and the Countess is teaching her, just like you and Father Williams, and there are medicine people in her family, just like mine—my grandfather would've known how to cure the King—

AP DAFYDD: Not. Another. Word. (*Breathing deeply before continuing.*) After everything we've taught you, all the time and energy I've put into trying to help you become good little Canadians. As a child in Wales, I was made to wear a piece of wood on a string around my neck if I were caught speaking Welsh in school. It would be passed on to the next child who was accused, sometimes by the other students, until the child left wearing it at the end of the day was beaten. The world out there is not kind to those who swim against the stream—I watched my father try. My parents became bitter people, shaking their fist at an Empire that didn't care. Let that be a lesson to embrace the education we're providing for you. (*To EVELYNE.*) Instead of breakfast, you'll be on extra laundry duty for the rest of the week. Beth, Susan, I presume you had nothing to do with this harebrained scheme?

BETH: I tried to explain that it was a bad idea—

AP DAFYDD: That's a relief. Susan?

                 SUSAN shakes her head.

                 Now, Act I, Scene 3, and I don't want to hear anyone else's good ideas, understood?

Enter FATHER WILLIAMS, running lines.

WILLIAMS: *(To himself, without an accent.)* "Farewell yong Lords, these warlike principles—" *(He stops.)* Is it my scene yet?

AP DAFYDD: Not yet, Father Williams, we've been delayed by a rather unfortunate incident—

BETH puts on her finest Ellen Terry, kicking her blanket around the room.

BETH: *(As Countess.)*
You know Hellen
I am a mother to you.

Silence, everyone turns to look at BETH. EVELYNE picks up the scene, the girls are holding their notebooks, but are mostly off-book. The playing of the scene is informed by the tension of BETH and EVELYNE's relationship.

EVELYNE: *(As Helena.)*
Mine honorable Mistris.

BETH: *(As Countess.)*
Nay I say a mother, 'tis often seene
Adoption strives with nature, and choice breedes
A native slip to us from forraine seedes:
I say I am your Mother.

EVELYNE: *(As Helena.)*
Pardon Madam.
The Count Rosillion cannot be my brother:
I am from humble, he from honored name.

BETH: *(As Countess.)*
Do you love my Sonne?

EVELYNE: *(As Helena.)*
                Doe not you love him Madam?

BETH: *(As Countess.)*
                Come, come, disclose:
                The state of your affection, for your passions
                Have to the full appeach'd.

EVELYNE: *(As Helena.)*
                Then I confesse
                Here on my knee—

AP DAFYDD: Kneel down. She is your superior, you her
                humble ward.

                          EVELYNE kneels.

EVELYNE: *(As Helena.)*
                I love your Sonne. Be not offended,
                For it hurts not him that he is lov'd of me.

BETH: *(As Countess.)*
                Had you not lately an intent, speake truely,
                To goe to Paris?

EVELYNE: *(As Helena.)*
                You know my Grandfather—

JEAN: Father.

EVELYNE: *(As Helena.)*
                My father left me some prescriptions
                Of rare and prov'd effects, Amongst the rest,
                There is a remedie, approv'd, set downe,
                To cure the desperate languishings whereof
                The King is render'd lost.

BETH: *(As Countess.)*
                He and his Phisitions
                Are of a minde, he, that they cannot helpe
                him:
                They, that they cannot helpe.

EVELYNE: *(As Helena.)*
                Would your honor
                But give me leave to trie successe, I'de
                venture
                The well lost life of mine, on his Graces cure.

                        The scene ends and they all stare in wonder.
                        Something magical has happened.

AP DAFYDD: Now you see, Evelyne, you didn't have to
                change a thing.

JOSEPH: That was Shakespeare?

WILLIAMS: How come I understood all of that?

AP DAFYDD: Because that's how Shakespeare is supposed
                to be done. *(To the students.)* Let's quit while
                we're ahead, shall we? Back to the dormitory.

                        FATHER WILLIAMS and MISS AP
                        DAFYDD exit as the students prepare to
                        follow them.

JEAN: Wow, that was pretty good, Evelyne!

JOSEPH: You too, Beth.

BETH: See what happens when you do what Miss
                Ap Dafydd tells you to?

EVELYNE: Guess I fooled you, too; my grampa was with
                me the whole time, with his medicines.

BETH: You're going to get us all in trouble.

SUSAN: They see what they want to see.

BETH: If she finds out she'll be furious!

EVELYNE: Then go and tell her and maybe I won't get
                lunch for a week either!

                        EVELYNE storms off, leaving BETH more
                        and more isolated from the group.

JOSEPH: Beth, isn't there room for both ways?

BETH: I don't want to get my head shaved.

>   *BETH storms off, leaving JOSEPH, JEAN,*
>   *and SUSAN.*

Transition 1.10-1.11

>   *A spirit image appears on one of the*
>   *chalkboards.*

Scene 1.11

>   *In the barn, by the goat pens, JEAN recites*
>   *some of the King's lines. He discovers that*
>   *the rhythm of the iambic is the same as the*
>   *round dance beat and starts to incorporate*
>   *the text with the dance.*

JEAN: *(As the King, no accent.)*
                     Tis onely title thou disdainst in her, the which
                     I can build up: strange is it that our bloods
                     Of colour, waight, and heat, pour'd all
                     together,

>   *JOSEPH enters with a bucket of alfalfa.*

                     Would quite confound distinction: yet stands
                     off
                     In differences so mightie.

JOSEPH: You got a death wish, or something?

JEAN: Evelyne's right. That horse thing that Ap
                     Daffy made us do? It's the same as our round
                     dance beat.

JOSEPH: Is that also what you think about when you
                     play hockey, 'cause that would explain a lot!

JEAN: We made the finals. We're playing Titsworth
                     in two weeks!

JOSEPH: Well, Evelyne's idea doesn't work for Bertram. You can't be white and Indian at the same time.

JEAN: Welcome to my world.
"Frémissant dans le calme où je marche établi
J'aurai la gloire aussi d'endurer un outrage."

JEAN waits for JOSEPH to respond. Receiving no response, he continues.

JEAN: That's Louis Riel. He reminds me of the King.

JOSEPH: You know who reminds *me* of the King? Principal Clarke—making some of the students get married, especially the ones who don't have anywhere to go. God, I hate this place.

JEAN: At least Bertram stands up for what he believes in. Like you do...

Beat.

JOSEPH: Not a lot of half-breeds get sent here. What happened with you?

JEAN: My mama had to leave the reserve after she married a white guy, but he took off after I came along. When I started doing well in school, the white folks in town told the Indian agent my mama was a drunk, which isn't true. Can't have a smart Indian around. I got sent here four years ago, "for my own good." My mama still cleans their houses and does their washing so she can make enough money to bring me home every summer.

JEAN begins a round dance again. JOSEPH joins in. They both get into dancing and saying the lines as the goats bleat in amusement.

JEAN: Tis onely title thou disdainst in her, the which
                        I can build up:

JOSEPH/
JEAN: Strange is it that our bloods
                        Of colour, waight, and heat, pour'd all
                        together,
                        Would quite confound distinction, yet stands
                        off
                        In differences *(JOSEPH stops abruptly; JEAN
                        finishes the line alone.)* so mightie.

JOSEPH: Don't get the idea that you're a *real* Indian or
                        anything.

JEAN: Wouldn't think of it.

Transition 1.11-1.12

                        *EVELYNE animates one of the chalkboards
                        with drawing of a plant.*

                        MISS AP DAFYDD erases it.

Scene 1.12

                        *The following Thursday, in rehearsal,
                        all are gathered. The girls have stopped
                        wearing their blankets and everyone has
                        memorized their lines.*

AP DAFYDD: *(Noticing the pouch.)*
                        Evelyne, what do you have there?

EVELYNE: *(Referring to her pouch.)*
                        I made it... something to carry Helena's...
                        things.

JOSEPH: From a scrap of leather MacFarlane didn't
                        need.

BETH opens her mouth to speak. JOSEPH looks at her with panic in his eyes.

AP DAFYDD: Good initiative. In fact, we should start a list of props, Beth, you can manage that. And!

BETH shrinks back and remains silent. FATHER WILLIAMS puts on his crown.

WILLIAMS   *(As the King, with French accent.)*
We thanke you maiden—

AP DAFYDD: We talked about this!

WILLIAMS: He's the King of France.

AP DAFYDD: No! In Shakespeare, it doesn't matter where you're from, everyone speaks with a proper English accent.

SUSAN: Is that how they perform it in Wales?

AP DAFYDD: Well… um… I…

JOSEPH: I like it.

The others, except BETH, nod or speak in agreement. "I like it too," "Sounds good," "Me, too."

AP DAFYDD: At this rate we'll give the League of Nations a run for their money. Now, where were we?

WILLIAMS: In my court. In France.

AP DAFYDD: And!

EVELYNE: *(As Helena, with British accent throughout but with much less Ellen Terry-style acting.)*
What I can doe, can doe no hurt to try.
And know I thinke, and thinke I know most sure,
My Art is not past power, nor you past cure.

> *FATHER WILLIAMS is deep in thought trying to remember his next line. BETH grows increasingly agitated.*

SUSAN: *(Aside)* What's that smell?

> *JOSEPH and JEAN repress giggles.*

WILLIAMS: *(As the King, with a French accent.)*
Methinks in thee some blessed spirit doth speak
His powerfull sound, within a... within a... damn it!

AD DAFYDD: Father Williams!

JEAN: ...within an organ weake:
Sweet prac—

WILLIAMS: I didn't call for line!

AP DAFYDD: Jean, only give the line if someone calls for it.

JEAN: Sorry.

EVELYNE: *(As Helena.)*
If I break time, unpitied let me die,
But if I helpe, what doe you promise me.

> *SUSAN is gesturing about the terrible smell.*

WILLIAMS: *(As the King.)*
Make thy demand.

EVELYNE: *(As Helena.)*
Then shalt thou give me with thy kingly hand
What husband in thy power I will command.

> *FATHER WILLIAMS offers his hand to be kissed, but EVELYNE shakes it.*

AP DAFYDD: And they exit... let's say stage left.

EVELYNE exits SL, FATHER WILLIAMS SR.

Your other left, Father Williams.

WILLIAMS: I'm all turned around.

AP DAFYDD: Helena is really coming to life, Evelyne.

BETH: Miss Ap Dafydd...

                The other students hold their breath.

                I don't feel very well, may I be excused?

AP DAFYDD: Straight to the dormitory, then.

                BETH exits, dejected.

                Now, Father Williams, I have a few notes for you.

                She pulls him aside to give him some discreet direction.

EVELYNE: That was close, I thought Beth was going to rat me out about my medicine pouch.

JEAN: I feel bad for her.

JOSEPH: Maybe it's good she's not Ap Daffy's pet anymore.

SUSAN: So much for brotherly love.

                JOSEPH freezes.

EVELYNE: We're not going to tell anyone.

SUSAN: Your secret's safe with us.

JEAN: I swear on my skates.

                JOSEPH relaxes.

SUSAN:	What was that smell? I almost choked to death.
JEAN:	You don't know?! Father Williams farts when he's nervous. The boys in the first three pews of the chapel call them —
JEAN/JOSEPH:	— "the trenches."
JEAN:	Mustard gas's got nothing on him.
JOSEPH:	He's scared of public speaking.
EVELYNE:	But he's a priest!

> *They look over to the teachers; they both have their lips puckered up and are massaging their jaws as MISS AP DAFYDD tries to teach FATHER WILLIAMS how to make the trilled "R" sound for the French accent on the word "brother."*

AP DAFYDD/ WILLIAMS:	Brrr, brrr, brrrrrodeurrrrr.
SUSAN:	We're never gonna get a new roof.

Transition 1.12-1.13

> *A spirit image appears on one of the chalkboards.*

Scene 1.13

> *It's a cold, late afternoon in mid-March. EVELYNE, JOSEPH, and SUSAN are helping to fix the vandalized fence.*

SUSAN:	Funny how the teachers can hear us tip-toeing down the hall but couldn't hear the entire fence being smashed to smithereens.

Unseen by the others, BETH enters upstage carrying a few apples intended as a peace offering, but she hides when she hears her name.

JOSEPH: Do you think Beth's still mad at me?

EVELYNE: I think she's afraid of getting into trouble.

JOSEPH: Something you're pretty good at.

SUSAN chuckles.

EVELYNE: I've been here a year and I still don't get this place.

JOSEPH: Try seven!

EVELYNE: I really miss my family.

JOSEPH: I can't quite remember what mine looks like.

SUSAN: Join the club.

EVELYNE: Ake'nistèn:ha wa'akote'nièn:ten ne... *(My mom fought to...)* Sorry, my mom fought to keep my older brothers and me in day school on our reserve but as soon as she died my father sent me here. He was here for ten years and said going to this school made him the successful businessman he is today.

JOSEPH: Sounds like your mother was very strong.

EVELYNE: Oh, you don't wanna mess with a Mohawk woman, if you know what's good for you.

JOSEPH: Understood.

JEAN enters out of breath, with a black eye and a bandage on his nose.

JEAN: They've only found four of the goats.

SUSAN: If Principal Clarke's face gets any redder, they'll think he's one of us. *(Seeing JEAN's nose.)* Wow, Jean! Do you get beat up in every game?

JEAN: Yeah, pretty much. But this time it was one of us. Billy was mad Father Williams put me in the starting lineup for the big game instead of him.

EVELYNE: Ouch.

JEAN: At least we ended the streak, we got a trophy and everything!

JOSEPH: And a smashed-up fence.

SUSAN: The webbe of our life really is of a mingled yarn.

JEAN: *(As Parolles, with a cockney accent.)*
Go to, thou art a wittie foole, I have found thee.

SUSAN: *(As Clown, speaking like her Uncle Clyde.)*
Did you finde me in your selfe, sir, or were you taught to finde me? The search sir was profitable, and much Foole may you find in you, even to the world's pleasure, and the encrease of laughter.

They all break into a fit of laughter.

JOSEPH: If they won't let Helena be Mohawk, they're not gonna let the Clown be...

SUSAN: My Uncle Clyde?

JOSEPH: You don't remember your parents, but you remember your uncle?

SUSAN: He always made me laugh. Maybe if I keep pretending to be Indian, I'll learn how to be one.

JEAN: You will always be Indian.

EVELYNE: Whether you know who they are or not, your ancestors are always inside you.

              FATHER WILLIAMS runs on wielding a hockey stick.

WILLIAMS: Did they come this way?!

              They look at him perplexed.

              The trip of goats! Wait, what are you boys and girls doing together?

JOSEPH: We're... rehearsing!

WILLIAMS: Glad to see this change of attitude. And Delorme, don't you pay any attention to what was painted on that fence, we won fair and square, ya hear?

JEAN: Yes, Coach!

              FATHER WILLIAMS runs out. SUSAN picks up a broken fence board and reads it.

SUSAN: "Dirty Indians use dirty tricks."

              EVELYNE picks up another one.

EVELYNE: "We'll get you cheaters!"

SUSAN: I wonder what they'll think when they find out the King and Queen are coming here and not to the Academy for Worthless Tits.

JEAN: Then we'd better have something good to show them.

JOSEPH: You're worse than Ap Daffy!

EVELYNE: We haven't even done the part where Helena says goodbye to her new husband.

(As Helena, flirtatiously and without an accent.)
I am not worthie of the wealth I own,
Nor dare I say 'tis mine: and yet it is,
But like a timorous theefe, most fain would
steale
What law does vouch mine owne.

JOSEPH   *(As Bertram, without an accent.)*
What would you have?

EVELYNE: *(As Helena. She gets closer, JOSEPH is becoming
more nervous.)*
I would not tell you what I would my Lord:
Faith yes,
Strangers and foes do sunder, and not kisse.

> *EVELYNE kisses JOSEPH. All are
> stunned.*

JEAN: Wait. What? Stop, stop, stop, that's not in the
script, is it? No, I'm sure I never read that in
the script. They don't kiss, do they? Do they?

EVELYNE: Well, that's what she's saying, isn't it? "Most
fain would steal what law does vouch
mine own." She wants to steal a kiss from
her husband, which she deserves, because
they're married, by law. I thought that was
obvious.

JEAN: If only Shakespeare wrote stage directions.

> *Beat.*

JOSEPH: I think we should keep it.

> *After they exit, BETH emerges and
> aggressively takes a few bites of an apple
> before exiting.*

Transition 1.13-1.14

> *MISS AP DAFYDD animates the central chalkboard; "Today's rehearsal; Act III, Scene II."*

Scene 1.14

> *Classroom late March, all the students are gathered in the classroom with MISS AP DAFYDD. A second bucket has been added. We hear a constant drip as spring's arrival is melting the snow on the roof.*

EVELYNE: *(As Helena, with British accent.)*
Who ever shoots at Bertram, I set him there.
Who ever charges on his forward brest
I am the Caitiffe that do hold him too't;
And though I kill him not, I am the cause
His death was so effected: Better 'twere
I met the ravine Lyon when he roar'd
With sharpe constraint of hunger: better 'twere,
That all the miseries which nature owes
Were mine at once. No Bertram come thou home.

> *All are stunned at the passion of her performance.*

BETH: Miss Ap Dafydd, Evelyne is, is... cheating!

AP DAFYDD: Whatever do you mean, Beth?

BETH: She's pretending that Helena is Mohawk.

AP DAFYDD: Oh, don't be ridiculous, I could tell if she were doing *that*.

JOSEPH: What difference does it make to you, Beth?

They all look at JOSEPH.

BETH: *(To MISS AP DAFYDD.)* I tried to warn you, but no one listens to me.

AP DAFYDD: So it's true, Evelyne?

EVELYNE nods.

To Principal Clarke's office right now!

JEAN: Evelyne's not the only one. My Parolles is Métis.

SUSAN: And I'm playing the Clown as my Uncle Clyde.

AP DAFYDD: That's it—for your own good, we're cancelling the performance. Now none of you will get to perform in a proper play, Principal Clarke will never let me direct Shakespeare again, and the school's roof will likely collapse and kill us all in our sleep.

FATHER WILLIAMS bursts in waving a newspaper.

WILLIAMS: Hang on to your hats! You won't believe it, but Mrs. Macbeth's article says that we're "revolutionizing Shakespeare," making it "uniquely Canadian." She thinks the King and Queen will love it. Principal Clarke has already received a dozen letters requesting tickets from prominent locals to the "Indian Shakespeare." We'll have to add more seats to the auditorium. We might have to move it outside to accommodate all the new donors.

Beat, no one responds.

Don't you get it, we're gonna be a hit!

Blackout—Intermission.

ACT II

Scene 2.1

> *As the lights shift to black, we hear the sound of a medium-sized group of children singing the following to the tune of "The Maple Leaf Forever."*

Our days are long, our hair is short
Frost blows through the window panes.
We never get enough to eat
A lashing if you complain.
By day we toil upon the farm
By night so cold we shiver.
And if they hear us speak our tongue,
We're forced to clean the shitter.

> *Lights come up on the continuation of the end of Act I, FATHER WILLIAMS is midway through the article.*

WILLIAMS: *(Reading the article in the* Ottawa Citizen.*)* "As every corner of the country is deep in preparation for the first visit of a British King and Queen to North America, I am most uplifted by the weekly rehearsals of the students at an Anglican Indian Residential School in northern Ontario. It is refreshing to know that upon the visit of Their Majesties, Canada, oft seen as host but not as birthplace of culture, will make them a uniquely Canadian cultural offering; Indian Shakespeare."

AP DAFYDD: *(She grabs the paper.)* Let me see that.

JOSEPH:	*(Aside to EVELYNE.)* "Indian Shakespeare," huh?
BETH:	What else does it say?
AP DAFYDD:	"Spearheaded by their intrepid English teacher, Miss Sian Ap Dafydd, the students will present *All's Well That Ends Well* to Their Majesties. Father Williams, an enthusiastic clergyman..."
WILLIAMS:	That's me!
AP DAFYDD:	"...was skeptical of the idea when it was first presented; 'I've never been very keen on plays, more of a hockey man myself.'"
WILLIAMS:	That's true!
AP DAFYDD:	"But I'm starting to understand the appeal."
WILLIAMS:	I really am!
AP DAFYDD:	"and so are *his* students; 'Shakespeare's words allow me to express who I am,' describes Evelyne, the young student playing Helena, 'Miss Ap Dafydd encouraged us to borrow from our own life experiences...'" When did I do that?
EVELYNE:	You told us—well, you quoted Ellen Terry—
SUSAN:	More than once!
AP DAFYDD:	*Dame* Ellen Terry... I feel faint.
BETH:	Let me help you, Miss Ap Dafydd. *(BETH takes the paper.)* "Their primitive life experiences will colour this production and make it of this place. One can imagine the skins and feathers that will be gathered for the costumes and the sound of the drums that will give it its 'savage flair.'"

AP DAFYDD: This can't be happening. Evelyne, what did you say to that woman?

EVELYNE: You were in the room with me, Miss Ap Dafydd.

WILLIAMS: Beth, give it here.

She does.

"Refreshingly, the burden of imitating our British brethren, that so often hampers the players of the Dominion Drama Festival, is of little use to these students. Perhaps the play is *indeed* the thing, wherein we'll catch the conscience of the King."

BETH/
AP DAFYDD: *Hamlet*; Act 2, Scene 2.

JEAN: I guess there *will* be dancing in this play after all!

Transition 2.1-2.2

EVELYNE draws a plant on a chalkboard.

JEAN writes "Dear Mama, did you get my letter?" on a chalkboard.

BETH erases the text on the central chalkboard: "Today's rehearsal; Act III, Scene II."

Scene 2.2

Later that evening, MISS AP DAFYDD and FATHER WILLIAMS are in his study arguing about next steps.

WILLIAMS: All I am suggesting, Shane—

AP DAFYDD: Miss Ap Dafydd to you—

WILLIAMS: All I am suggesting… Shane, is that we must consider the circumstances.

AP DAFYDD: For years I was ridiculed by your predecessor Father Becker for "wasting my time" teaching Shakespeare to my students. And now you're asking me to compromise everything I have fought for by coercing me into an "Indian Shakespeare"?

WILLIAMS: I understand your reticence, I'm merely asking myself, "How bad can it get?"

AP DAFYDD: This from someone who would rather watch *HMS Pinafore* than *Henry VI, Part II*!

WILLIAMS: We have a duty to the school.

AP DAFYDD: Don't talk to me about dedication, Father Williams. The longer they hang onto their... ways... the more they will suffer in the long run. My father became a penniless drunk, singing old Welsh songs to the end. I made my commitment to ensure that our young Indian wards have a chance in this world when I was eighteen years old, unlike you who waltzed in here less than a year ago! But even the strength I have gathered these thirty years of working in less than adequate surroundings could not have prepared me for this outrageous request.

WILLIAMS: Why are people in the theatre so dramatic?

AP DAFYDD: I am not dramatic, I am sensitive!

WILLIAMS: Miss Ap Dafydd, the Lord has provided us with an opportunity to prosper at a time when the pending war compounds our financial insecurity, on top of the lingering hardships of the Depression. There may not even *be* jobs for us in the near future, let alone a functional building, if we do not carefully weigh our options. What could be the harm of giving this a go?

AP DAFYDD: The souls of our children for one.

WILLIAMS: We're not asking them to *be* Indians, but rather simply to *play* Indians. The idea of seeing real live Indians, dressed up as Indians on stage, has sparked the intrigue of our theatre audience. Curiosity may have killed the cat, but it's also doubled our ticket sales.

AP DAFYDD: And where, pray tell, are we to find Indian costumes?

WILLIAMS: The Women's Auxiliary has volunteered to make them! Apparently, they have an expert amongst them. Of course, I will arrange for each costume to have a cross sewn into it, to offset any pagan... we'll need all the prayers we can get.

AP DAFYDD: We can turn to the Archbishop! He's already booked front row seats for himself and several prominent priests from the area.

> *An audible fart is heard.*

WILLIAMS: He's... oh... oh no, no. Oh, no, oh no, oh no!

> *MISS AP DAFYDD does her best to calm FATHER WILLIAMS.*

AP DAFYDD: Long deep breaths in and out. IN and OUT. IN and OUT.

WILLIAMS: (*Catching his breath.*) I won't get my own parish until I prove to Archbishop Owen that I have overcome my... ummm... uneasiness with public speaking.

AP DAFYDD: Your "uneasiness with"—

> *FATHER WILLIAMS releases another audible toot.*

...do you mean to tell me that those... unfortunate smells that occasionally emanate from— *(She suddenly catches a whiff of it and retreats.)* are as a result of your nerves?

WILLIAMS: We all have crosses to bear.

AP DAFYDD: And mine is to help with your flatulence?!

WILLIAMS: I was relying on your expertise as a director to help me vanquish my fear of crowds, the Archbishop would hear of my triumph, and BINGO, my own parish! But I didn't anticipate him actually coming to northern Ontario!

AP DAFYDD: You're more concerned about performing in front of the Archbishop than you are of the King?

WILLIAMS: Now that you mention it...

> *Another toot is heard.*

AP DAFYDD: Well, let's start by figuring out what an "Indian Shakespeare" is.

WILLIAMS: I suggest that we tighten our defensive strategy and then pull out the old dump-and-chase.

AP DAFYDD: I don't even want to ask.

Scene 2.3

> *Early April. Everyone is gathered for their first rehearsal of the "Indian Shakespeare." A cold tension permeates the room. Finally, JOSEPH speaks.*

JOSEPH:	But being Ojibwe is different from being Mohawk!
EVELYNE:	And Mohawk is different from being Cree!
SUSAN:	And being Indian is different from... not being an Indian.
AP DAFYDD:	Accuracy isn't important—it's a Shakespeare play!
EVELYNE:	It's important to us.
BETH:	*(To EVELYNE.)* Everything isn't always about your / grand-father.
AP DAFYDD:	We're not here to tell everyone's singular story, it's about the characters.
JOSEPH:	Then what makes this an Indian Shakespeare?
AP DAFYDD:	Isn't there some kind of generic Indian concept that you can all agree on?
	The students are speechless until JEAN breaks the silence.
JEAN:	Let's start with what we know.
	JEAN grabs a piece of chalk and is about to write on the board when he decides to offer it to FATHER WILLIAMS instead.
	Coach?
	FATHER WILLIAMS smiles, grabs the piece of chalk, and starts putting diagrams on the chalkboard similar to those of a hockey play.
	Helena is a Mohawk girl who was taught how to use the medicines by her father.

FATHER WILLIAMS draws a stick figure with a little dress with "Helena" written above it. JEAN draws a stick figure of a man beside her with the words "Medicine Man" written above it.

SUSAN: And Parolles is a half-breed... who couldn't grow up on his reserve because his mama married a white man.

JEAN draws another stick figure, FATHER WILLIAMS writes "half-breed" beside it and then colours in half the face.

EVELYNE: And the clown is a joke-cracking Cree man.

WILLIAMS: But isn't Susan playing...

JEAN writes "Clown" and then "Susan?" beside it.

JOSEPH: Our play should take place before the white man arrived on our land!

JEAN: But then Parolles couldn't be Métis! Unless he was half Viking...

JEAN crosses out "breed" and writes "Viking" below "half" and adds some horns.

AP DAFYDD: *(Putting her foot down.)* Our play will be set in present day; a fictional Ojibwe Indian reserve situated close to a thriving white settlement.

JEAN draws a square for the reserve and writes the word "Ojibwe" and then FATHER WILLIAMS draws another square and writes the word "Whites."

WILLIAMS: *(Drawing the church and wigwam inside the Ojibwe square.)* With a church next to a wigwam.

JOSEPH: *(Throwing his hands up in the air.)* And we're back where we started!

BETH: Miss Ap Dafydd, none of the Indian characters in our play are Ojibwe.

                   FATHER WILLIAMS erases the Ojibwe square.

SUSAN: Except for the Countess and Bertram.

                   Everyone's attention turns to SUSAN.

BETH: But don't they live in the white town?

SUSAN: In our play the Countess and Bertram live in the white town but they're really from the Ojibwe reserve. Like me, the Countess had to marry, and she moved to town with her husband after they left Residential School.

                   JEAN writes "Countess" and "Bertram" by the square for the White Town.

                   When her husband dies, she could go back to the reserve, but she isn't sure where she belongs anymore.

AP DAFYDD: She belongs in white society, Susan.

SUSAN: That is exactly what Principal Clarke wrote in the town paper last week. I read the newspapers that line the crates delivered to the kitchen. *(To MISS AP DAFYDD.)* Now I understand what you mean; that reading will be good for us, because I've discovered all kinds of things! In Principal Clarke's monthly reports, he talks about how successful the school is at "killing the Indian" in us. And it's true! I've been here since my parents died when I was four years old. I don't even know where I'm from, so I don't fit in anywhere.

Bertram and the Countess are the same. Which explains why Bertram's a... well, you know... a little bit of a...

JOSEPH: Father Williams, an Ojibwe reserve next to the white town!

> *FATHER WILLIAMS hands him the chalk and JOSEPH draws a circle with the word "Ojibwe" in it. EVELYNE grows increasingly withdrawn throughout.*

SUSAN: And a Cree reserve for the clown!

> *SUSAN writes "Cree Reserve" and then draws a circle around it and "Clown" and "Susan?".*

BETH: This is confusing.

AP DAFYDD: We run the risk of losing our audience.

JEAN: More confusing than *All's Well That Ends Well*?

JOSEPH: But if Bertram is Ojibwe, whose war is he fighting?

JEAN: That's obvious; he's fighting for the white town who want more Indian land.

BETH: But Miss Ap Dafydd—

> *FATHER WILLIAMS refers to the space between the Cree reserve circle and the White square and adds a question mark to it.*

WILLIAMS: You mean this space here, that no one's using?

EVELYNE: It's traditional territory; hunting and fishing land.

WILLIAMS: But they aren't actually living there; the town has every right to put it to good use.

JOSEPH: So, Bertram is helping the white town get Cree land?

AP DAFYDD: What has land got to do with our Indian Shakespeare?

JOSEPH: Everything's always about land.   EVELYNE: Everything!

JEAN: Bertram doesn't know who he is anymore, that's what our Indian Shakespeare is really about.

SUSAN: Which is why Bertram looks down on Helena.

BETH: Because she grew up on a reserve?

AP DAFYDD: John A. MacDonald said it himself, if you remain on the reserves, even if you are educated, you are "simply a savage who can read and write." We're trying to elevate you, for your own salvation.

WILLIAMS: The King could be Sir John A. MacDonald! He was, after all, Canada's first great leader. Though I'd have to relinquish my crown.

He draws a head with a crown on it and adds "Sir John A." next to it.

JEAN: Or, maybe the King could be Louis Riel?

WILLIAMS: You mean that megalomaniac from Manitoba?

JEAN: Some people consider him a hero.

BETH: Aren't they both dead?

JOSEPH: Riel was a half-breed, so the King in our play would still be part French.

JEAN: You could keep your accent.

AP DAFYDD: John A. did have a nasty reputation with the
               bottle...

BETH: But Riel was Catholic!

WILLIAMS: So was the King of France.

SUSAN: What's the matter, Evelyne, you gonna miss
               your British accent?

EVELYNE: Helena is Mohawk.

               They all look at the chalkboard realizing
               they have not included EVELYNE.

JEAN: Maybe your father was Mohawk and your
               mother Ojibwe.

               JEAN writes "Mohawk" above "Medicine
               Man" and "Mom" in the Ojibwe circle,
               with a heart between them.

JOSEPH: When your father dies, you come north in
               search of your mother.

               JOSEPH draws a dotted line that links
               Helena to the Ojibwe reserve.

EVELYNE: But no one knows where she is!

SUSAN: Like Jenny.

EVELYNE: And Heather, Dorothy...

JOSEPH: Ethan, Karl, Jeremy...

JEAN: Logan... Charlie...

BETH: And Alice...

AP DAFYDD: Louis Riel... that's a compromise I can live
               with and you would look smashing in a
               moustache, Father Williams.

MISS AP DAFYDD crosses out the crown and draws a moustache on the face.

BETH: And what are the rest of us supposed to wear?

AP DAFYDD: The spectators *would* be disappointed if you aren't all dressed in "skins and feathers."

WILLIAMS: All of us?!

JEAN: But Louis—

SUSAN: *(To FATHER WILLIAMS.)* They might ask for their money back—

JEAN: Just saying that Louis Riel didn't—

AP DAFYDD: You do have the Archbishop to consider—

BETH: I don't understand, Miss Ap Dafydd, you said there was only one way to do Shakespeare!

AP DAFYDD: Mrs. Macbeth has forced our hand, so we have to be careful not to... tip the canoe... not that I've ever been in one.

BETH: *(To MISS AP DAFYDD.)* But you said…

BETH runs out of the room.

JOSEPH: *(Begins to run out after her.)* Beth, wait!

AP DAFYDD: Joseph Summers, sit back down!

JOSEPH does, and MISS AP DAFYDD exits after BETH.

WILLIAMS: I suppose, as the most important character in the play, I'll do what it takes to make this show a success. God help me, playing a half-breed!

JEAN: Louis Riel didn't wear skins and feathers!

WILLIAMS: Clearly, we must all make sacrifices, Delorme.

FATHER WILLIAMS erases "John A." and writes "Louie Real." FATHER WILLIAMS exits, and JEAN then erases "Louie Real" and re-writes "Louis Riel."

Scene 2.4

BETH huddled in a nook of the staircase. MISS AP DAFYDD enters.

AP DAFYDD: Beth, this is not like you.

BETH: You said Shakespeare can only be done one way and now Father Williams is wearing a moustache and we have to be Indians, even though we've been told that we should be ashamed of who we are.

AP DAFYDD: Shhhh! I admit, it is a rather confounding situation.

BETH: Do you still like me?

AP DAFYDD: Beth I... I care deeply for all of my students. It is my job to ensure that you leave this school with hope for a brighter future.

BETH: You're my only friend.

AP DAFYDD: Come now, Beth, you have friends.

BETH: I had Alice. The other girls spit in my hair and call me names because you pay more attention to me. But now Evelyne's your favourite. I thought I was special to you.

AP DAFYDD: All the students are special to me, Beth. The Countess loves Helena and Bertram equally. "Which of them both
Is deerest to me, I have no skill in sence
To make distinction."

BETH:	Will you write to me after I graduate?
AP DAFYDD:	That depends on what you plan on doing.
BETH:	I want to continue school... like you told me I should. I want to be a teacher, but if Joe finds out, he'll insist I go home to our family...

BETH realizes too late what she has revealed.

AP DAFYDD:	Joseph is your brother?
BETH:	And he's going to be a wonderful Bertram!
AP DAFYDD:	The school's policy! Siblings interacting is absolutely forbidden. Why didn't you tell me?
BETH:	By the time Principal Clarke realizes, the King and Queen will already be here and—
AP DAFYDD:	Your secret has put the whole project in jeopardy.
BETH:	Helena disguises herself and convinces Diana to lure Bertram into... her bed and then she tricks him into... you know. But, all's well that ends well, so as long as it's for the greater good, then maybe withholding a bit of truth is okay sometimes.
AP DAFYDD:	Alright, I'll keep your secret, if you stop fighting this "Indian Shakespeare." It's not my cup of tea either, but... ugh.
BETH:	So you won't tell anyone about me and Joe?
AP DAFYDD:	Joe and me—God help me, no. Now back to rehearsal.

Transition 2.4-2.5

> *SUSAN animates one of the chalkboards with: "I was here."*
>
> *FATHER WILLIAMS erases "Dear Mama, did you get my letter?"*
>
> *JOSEPH erases the central chalkboard with images from 2.3.*

Scene 2.5

> *Mid-April; everyone is gathered for rehearsal. JOSEPH, BETH, and SUSAN, in character, ambush JEAN as Parolles and blindfold him.*

JEAN:
(As Parolles.)
O ransome, ransome, Do not hide mine eyes.

> *Beat.*

AP DAYFDD: Father Williams, the drums would start here.

WILLIAMS: I'm still working on it. But... well, you've met Sergeant Berhn. The drums belong to the Cadets, so only the marching band has his permission.

BETH: Maybe the drummers could be part of our play?

AP DAFYDD: That's the kind of thinking we need. Now back to the French army—I mean the soldiers—I mean the folks from the white town.

EVELYNE: I can make the sound of a drum for now?

> *MISS AP DAFYDD nods, EVELYNE begins making the sound of a drum.*

SUSAN: *(As the First Soldier.)*
                Our leader is content to spare thee yet,
                Haply thou mayst informe
                Something to save thy life.

JEAN: *(As Parolles.)*
                O let me live, I will confesse what I know
                without constraint, for I know the young
                Bertram to be a dangerous and lascivious boy.

BETH: *(As the Lord; aside to Bertram.)*
                This is your devoted friend sir.

SUSAN: *(As the First Soldier.)*
                I perceive sir by our Leaders looks, wee shall
                be faine to hang you.

JEAN: *(As Parolles.)*
                I would repent out the remainder of Nature
                i'th bush, so I may live.

SUSAN: *(As the First Soldier.)*
                There is no remedy sir: you that have so
                traitorously made such pestiferous reports of
                a man very nobly held, so you must die.

JEAN: *(As Parolles.)*
                O please let me live, or let me see my death.

SUSAN: *(As the First Soldier.)*
                That shall you, and take your leave of all your
                friends.

                *SUSAN takes off his blindfold as EVELYNE
                stops drumming. JEAN speaks the following
                text both as Parolles and as himself to his
                fellow students.*

JEAN: Who cannot be crush'd with a plot?
                Yet am I thankfull: if my heart were great
                'Twould burst at this: simply the thing I am
                Shall make me live: and so Parolles live

Safest in shame: being fool'd, by fool'rie thrive;
There's place and means for every man alive.

Silence.

AP DAFYDD: Jean, that was simply... All of you. Simply...

Evening bell rings.

We'll have to leave it there.

MISS AP DAFYDD exits.

EVELYNE: Sheesh Susan, you sure know how to play a good bully.

The students, about to exit, stop in response to EVELYNE's comment. FATHER WILLIAMS lingers.

SUSAN: We just pretended we were those hockey players from Titsworth. Right, Beth?

JOSEPH acknowledges JEAN with a gesture of friendship. They all file out. A letter drops from FATHER WILLIAMS' pocket as he exits.

JEAN reads the name on the envelope.

JEAN: "To Jean Delorme"

He opens the envelope and reads the letter.

"My d-i-r-is- Dirist son.
My first litter." Litter? Letter, my first letter.
"I sorry I let them take you from me. I still hear you cry as you go with the man.
I thinc of you evry breath.
Hope this yer you hav make frends.
The earth brings yellow fleurs early. They like your smile when I see them.

I practis my riting. And readin like you teach
me.
I practis my counting. I tell one of the woman
I clean for she not pay me what she say she
would. I laugh when she lurn I can count! Her
face!
My sore hands bring in white man money to
send to school to bring yu home. The north
wind comes thru my winduw but my hurt is
warm when I hold you this summer.
I love you.
Mama"

A small tear falls from JEAN's face.

Transition 2.5-2.6

*BETH animates a chalkboard with
practising her cursive writing: "She derives
her honesty."*

*FATHER WILLIAMS erases the chalk-
board with the text "I was here" and
EVELYNE'S drawing from the end of 2.1.*

Scene 2.6

*Late April, the middle of the night. We
find SUSAN alone in the girl's bathroom.
EVELYNE comes in wearing her medicine
pouch and carrying some cloths.*

EVELYNE: I can help.

SUSAN: With what?

EVELYNE: Two girls on their moon time gave me their
             extra rags.

SUSAN: I'm fine.

EVELYNE: I promise it won't hurt.

SUSAN: I'm fine, Evelyne, go away.

EVELYNE: If that infection gets worse, you'll have to go
                  to the infirmary.

> *SUSAN nods. EVELYNE goes to the sink
> and wets the cloths and then goes to her
> and gently peels away the newspaper strips
> SUSAN has put on her wound. She then
> takes some leaves from her medicine pouch.*

EVELYNE: Niawenhkó:wa teionerahtastaráthe *(big thank
                  you broad leaf plantain)*.

SUSAN: *(Referencing the medicines.)* What is that?

EVELYNE: Teionerahtastaráthe *(broad leaf plantain)*. It's
                  everywhere, so most people think it's a weed.

> *Throughout the following, EVELYNE
> places the leaves on the wound and drapes
> the wet cloths over them. SUSAN has a
> sharp intake of breath, doing everything
> not to cry.*

SUSAN: *(Repeating one of the words.)* Teionerahtas-
                  taráthe.

EVELYNE: *(Correcting her.)* Teionerahtastaráthe.

SUSAN: Teionerahtastaráthe.

EVELYNE: *(Correcting her, slowly.)* Teionerahtastaráthe.

SUSAN: Teionerahtastaráthe?

EVELYNE: Almost.

> *EVELYNE drapes a cloth over the leaves
> and then replaces the shoulder of SUSAN's
> nightgown.*

SUSAN: "Susan Blackbird, one more smart remark out
                  of you and..." Why can't I keep my mouth
                  shut?

EVELYNE: If he weren't the one in charge, I'd bury my fist in his face.

SUSAN: When I get out of here, no one's ever going to touch me like this again.

EVELYNE: (*Offering SUSAN some leaves.*) Here, take some in your hands and speak to it.

SUSAN: What do I say?

EVELYNE: My grampa taught me that when you pick the medicines you have to ask permission to use them. It's important to pray to the spirit of the plant, asking them to share their medicine. Teiethinonhwerá:ton (*We will give thanks and respect to*).

SUSAN: You're lucky you know so much.

EVELYNE: I'll teach you.

SUSAN: Still never gonna be mine.

EVELYNE: You'll figure it out.

               EVELYNE unwraps a ball of pine sap from her medicine pouch.

               This one's Tsonerahtase'kó:wa Orá:na (*white pine sap*). For the smaller cuts.

               She puts the pine sap on SUSAN's smaller cuts. It stings.

SUSAN: How would I say thank you?

EVELYNE: Niá:wen (*thank you*).

SUSAN: (*To EVELYNE.*) Niá:wen (*thank you*).

EVELYNE: Almost.

               SUSAN whispers to the leaves in her hands.

Transition 2.6-2.7

> *BETH finishes the previous line from the end of 2.5 with: "and achieves her goodness."*

> *On another chalkboard, JOSEPH writes: "gi-maaminonenimaa."*

> *On the central chalkboard, FATHER WILLIAMS writes: "A senseless help, when help past sense we deem."*

Scene 2.7

> *Early May. MRS. MACBETH, MISS AP DAFYDD and FATHER WILLIAMS are in the visitation room. SUSAN is secretly listening at the door.*

WILLIAMS: *(Producing a pamphlet.)* These pamphlets have put our whole endeavour in jeopardy.

AP DAFYDD: People have started requesting refunds.

MACBETH: Although anything royal related is selling like the dickens; a welcome distraction from Hitler's tirade against my father's people, I can't guarantee the article you've asked me to write will be enough.

WILLIAMS: They're circulating lies! *(Reading.)* "Savages bribe referee!", "Titsworth Academy swindled out of win." Don't believe a word of it, Mrs. Macbeth, there was no cheating in that championship game, I'll swear on my Bible!

MACBETH: How well do you know these Titsworth Academy folk?

WILLIAMS: A few attend our church in town—

AP DAFYDD: One owns the mill.

WILLIAMS: And of course, the goalie's father is the mayor.

MACBETH: I'm afraid the Titsworth wives, off the record of course, allude to a plot as thick as a Shakespearean play.

WILLIAMS: Titsworth wives?

MACBETH: An elite social committee I had the pleasure of meeting with this morning for tea. Surely you've not forgotten the tactic I revealed to you: if you want to know what the men are up to, simply ask the women—who tell me this storm has been brewing for some time.

                SUSAN bursts through the door.

SUSAN: It's true, all the recent letters to the editor are urging people to boycott our production in honour of the "upstanding young men at Titsworth."

MACBETH: And the editor's son is one of those "upstanding young men," if I'm not mistaken.

AP DAFYDD: *(To SUSAN.)* I told you to stop reading those!

WILLIAMS: Not to mention eavesdropping on private conversations!

                We hear a commotion outside the classroom. MISS AP DAFYDD scurries over to the door and ushers in the other four students who slink in.

JEAN: *(Shyly raising his hand.)* Lady Macbeth—

AP DAFYDD: Jean!

MACBETH: They only call me *that* when they think I'm out of earshot.

JEAN: *Mrs.* Macbeth; you can't let them do this!

MACBETH: As a journalist I have a responsibility to remain impartial.

WILLIAMS: Tell that to the Titsworth perjurers who printed these pamphlets!

AP DAFYDD: She's right, there's nothing she can do. Nothing any of us can do. All I wanted was a simple Shakespearean production... to celebrate the talent of these young thespians... Jean's Parolles would give Gielgud a run for his money... and now my directing career is over before it—

MACBETH: Miss Ap Dafydd, all hope is not lost. During a lively discussion, the Titsworth wives revealed that this would go away if... the trophy were returned.

                 That hits hard for everyone.

JOSEPH: We return the trophy and they let us do the play?

JEAN: Their streak lives on.

WILLIAMS: Scoundrels!

AP DAFYDD: Why would they go to all this trouble... it's just hockey!

EVERYONE
EXCEPT
AP DAFYDD: Just hockey!?!?

WILLIAMS: The boys were so very proud of their accomplishment!

EVELYNE: Everyone at the school was really happy...

JOSEPH: For once.

SUSAN: Principal Clarke cried.

BETH: So that's it. We won't be able to do our play!

JOSEPH: The kids at this school won't see us being the real... us-es.

AP DAFYDD: Unless your article...

MACBETH: When my husband died, I was faced with the realities of being a single mother. My dream of being a novelist didn't put food in the mouths of my two growing boys, but journalism did. I've had to report on all kinds of stories, some that I found fundamentally offensive, but sometimes, in order to redeem the circumstances you're dealt, you need to eat a certain amount of crow.

EVELYNE: Indian people know all about sacrifice.

BETH: Compromise.

SUSAN: Veritas!

                Everyone looks at SUSAN.

                It's the Titsworth Academy motto—pretty funny if you ask me.

                FATHER WILLIAMS turns to JEAN.

WILLIAMS: Well?

JEAN: If I had to choose, I think my mama would be happiest with us, being us. You know, in iambic pentameter and all.

                They all nod.

WILLIAMS: I'll handle it, Delorme.

JEAN: The guys on the team are gonna be so angry.

AP DAFYDD: Are you certain you're prepared to go through with this?

WILLIAMS: Even without a trophy, we're still champions.

MACBETH: Indeed. And to help grease the wheels of this negotiation, front row tickets to the event of the season for those Titsworth wives could really seal the deal.

Transition 2.7-2.8

> *A spirit image appears on one of the chalkboards.*
>
> *FATHER WILLIAMS erases "A senseless help when help past sense we deem" from the central chalkboard.*

Scene 2.8

> *Mid-May, and excitement is in the air. All are gathered to distribute the costumes. The five STUDENTS are loading in boxes and cardboard set pieces, with FATHER WILLIAMS directing traffic. MISS AP DAFYDD looks on expectantly.*

WILLIAMS: Over in the corners, lads, I mean boys, I mean boys and girls. Ahh, I just can't keep up with these modern times.

AP DAFYDD: The moment we have all been waiting for! Be careful, the women at the church have been working day and night to gather all that we need! I know having these costumes to play with will inspire you all.

WILLIAMS: I am anxious to try on my moustache.

Everyone begins to open the boxes and take out the items. Excitement quickly descends into disbelief from the students. A fake head dress, a fringed fake buckskin loin cloth, a ratty old wool blanket that even MISS AP DAFYDD has a reaction to.

SUSAN: Wow...

AP DAFYDD: My oh my, the women have outdone themselves. Absolutely stunning work! That blanket, however, is in less than adequate condition. Beth, I'll rely on you to take care of this.

EVELYNE: *(Holding up a fringed yoke with a painted pattern.)* Where did they get these designs from?

AP DAFYDD: Why does it matter? They're Indian designs.

JOSEPH: That have nothing to do with us.

SUSAN: *(Picking up the long wool braided wig and showing it to MISS AP DAFYDD.)* We're supposed to wear these?

AP DAFYDD: I told the women at the church that we needed long hair, since it is required, for your own salvation of course, that yours be cut.

JEAN: They're made of wool.

JOSEPH: Too bad you cut our hair in the first place...

EVELYNE: I feel sick.

WILLIAMS: *(Searching through the boxes.)* Has anyone seen my moustache?

SUSAN: Everyone will laugh at us.

AP DAFYDD: It's a comedy!

JEAN: That we want to make as realistic as possible.

JOSEPH: *(Holding up a second yoke.)* Is this what you meant when you said "Accuracy isn't important"?

AP DAFYDD: Our sold-out audience is expecting an Indian Shakespeare in less than a week. Without skins and feathers they're going to be very disappointed!

JEAN: I thought this was about us being us?

AP DAFYDD: This is as close as you'll get to being "real" Indians again.

EVELYNE: Braids or not, we're still treated like "real" Indians.

JEAN: I thought you liked my Parolles scene. I did that without a costume.

AP DAFYDD: The King of England is coming to our school! You're wearing these costumes!

JOSEPH: *(Holding up a wig.)* But I won't wear *this*!

WILLIAMS: *(Pulling out a moustache.)* This moustache isn't exactly what I had in mind either.

BETH: All right, Miss Ap Dafydd, we'll wear these wigs and costumes... if you convince Principal Clarke to let Joe go home.

> *The other students freeze. BETH and MISS AP DAFYDD have a momentary stand-off.*

AP DAFYDD: And you all agree to Beth's ultimatum?

> *The other students slowly nod in agreement. Eventually FATHER WILLIAMS joins in.*

Fine, I'll see what I can do.

WILLIAMS: How are you going to get Principal Clarke to
               agree?

AP DAFYDD: I'm not, but as the school's official liaison to
               the royal reception on behalf of the Women's
               Auxiliary, I know I can rely on you.

Transition 2.8-2.9

> *A spirit image appears on one of the
> chalkboards.*

Scene 2.9

> *Kitchen, BETH is peeling potatoes,
> JOSEPH enters.*

JOSEPH: I need to talk to you.

BETH: We can't.

JOSEPH: I'll meet you in the pantry, just tell them you
               ran out.

BETH: They won't let me go to the pantry alone!

> *JOSEPH picks up the potato bag and exits
> to the pantry.*

               I'm just getting more potatoes, I'll be right
               back.

> *BETH exits and joins JOSEPH in the
> pantry, no one follows.*

JOSEPH: Gaakaabishiikwe— *(Hawk woman)*

BETH: Don't call me that!

JOSEPH: You mean your real name?

> *She gives him a look.*

Okay. Beth. You were right, doing the play is worth it, I get to see my littl— my sister every week.

BETH: And your girlfriend.

JOSEPH: Evelyne? Pfff. She's not my girlfriend. Who told you that? Did she say that? Did she say something? Anything? Did she ask for me? Answer me in one word!

BETH: ...moron.

JOSEPH: Look, we don't have much time, I wanted to thank you for getting me out of this hellhole and I promise that as soon as you graduate I'm gonna find a way to get you home.

BETH: I'm not going home, Joe. Doing this play has made me realize that I want to be a teacher more than ever.

JOSEPH: But if you go to college you'll lose your status. Your rights.

BETH: We've already lost them. If I were a teacher, people would see what we're capable of. I'm proposing an idea to Miss Ap Dafydd for next year; Viola in *Twelfth Night* as a young Indian girl.

JOSEPH: You used to tell everyone that you were going to be a great hunter like me. I even helped you make a bow, remember that? Remember ni-maamaanaan *(our mother)* singing to us every day?

BETH: That was a long time ago, Joe.

JOSEPH: I still remember the first night we came here. You were only eight years old. When I asked Becker where they had taken you, he slapped me across the face for speaking

Anishinaabemowin. I just wanted to know where you were; I was supposed to protect you, I promised our parents that I would.

BETH: It's okay, Joe, we've survived, haven't we?

JOSEPH: But you don't want to come home. They've done that to you, Beth.

BETH: What would I do there? Our parents don't speak English and I don't speak our language anymore. The future is not back on the reserve for me.

JOSEPH: Don't say that, Gaakaabishiikwe (*Hawk woman*).

BETH: "It is in Us to plant our Honour, where We please to have it grow."

JOSEPH: A miniature ApDaffy in the making.

            BETH grabs the bag of potatoes.

BETH: Maybe it's better if when you go home next month, we never see each other again. That way I won't keep disappointing you for the rest of my life!

            She exits.

Transition 2.9-2.10

            MRS. MACBETH erases all of the chalkboards.

Scene 2.10

            Backstage, the students are prepping for their quick changes and arranging props, all in costumes and wigs, except for JOSEPH who holds his wig. We can hear a crowd gathering for the performance.

AP DAFYDD: My goodness, the blackflies out there in the audience are thicker than *The Collected Works of Shakespeare! (Smacks her neck.)* Has anyone seen Father Williams?

JEAN: I think he's still memorizing Act V!

> *Enter FATHER WILLIAMS in full regalia, with a Louis Riel moustache being held to his face with his index finger.*

WILLIAMS: I'm not sure I've got the hang of this holy gum.

AP DAFYDD: Spirit gum.

SUSAN: Amen.

> *He removes his finger and the moustache is attached to it and not his face. He promptly returns it to his upper lip. MISS AP DAFYDD tries to assist him, to no avail.*

AP DAFYDD: All the Titsworth mothers are as pleased as punch in their VIP seating, right next to Mrs. Macbeth and Archbishop Owen. Don't forget to project and trust the excellent work you've all done over these past five months.

> *We hear the fanfare, played by the marching band. FATHER WILLIAMS runs out.*

That's places. Father Williams?!

> *She runs after him.*

> *BETH, followed by some of the others, notices that JOSEPH still hasn't put on his wig.*

BETH: We made a deal, Joe.

> *JOSEPH hesitates and then puts it on. The all exit to begin the play.*

Scene 2.11

We witness the backstage action; people changing costumes, grabbing props, getting into their new character, exiting and entering upstage. We hear laughter, snippets of text including Bertram: "What it is, my good lord, the Chief Languishes of?" Clown: "A fistula, my Lord." Parolles: "Virginity is peevish, proud, idle, made of self love." King: "I would I had that corporall soundnesse now." Helena: "Of my dear fathers gifts stand chief in power." Clown: "It's like a barber's chair that fits all buttocks." King: "Why, then, young Bertram, take her, she's thy wife." Bertram: "I'll to the wars, she to her single sorrow." Countess: "When you see my son, To tell him that his sword can never win." Parolles: "It will come to pass that every Braggart shall be found an ass."

Time passes, four acts and many characters worth. EVELYNE and JOSEPH are left alone backstage.

JOSEPH goes to kiss EVELYNE, she pulls back.

EVELYNE: Joseph, I...

JOSEPH: Sorry, I didn't mean...

EVELYNE: No, it's not that... Hà:ke wahí, Evelyne... *(Expression of frustration in Kanien'kéha.)* I'm joining the army.

JOSEPH: You're what?

EVELYNE: I want to get my nursing certificate. I'll make my Raksótha *(Grampa)* proud.

JOSEPH: But Evelyne, I... what about... aren't we... it's dangerous.

EVELYNE: I survived this place.

> *JEAN enters backstage followed by SUSAN and BETH.*

JEAN: *(To EVELYNE and JOSEPH.)* Act V, scene 1, you're up!

> *The drumbeat begins.*

JOSEPH: *(To the students.)* Wait!

> *They all look at him. JOSEPH slowly takes off his wig. SUSAN follows, then EVELYNE and JEAN, leaving BETH undecided, until she finally follows. SUSAN begins tearing off the fringe, Indian design and accents, leaving a neutral base. The others join in, creating a pile of wigs and costume pieces that they remove when they exit to begin Act V.*

Scene 2.12

> *The perspective shifts to the outdoor performance of Act V of the "Indian Shakespeare." Clouds are hanging low with the threat of rain.*

Scene 1

> *We hear sounds of drums in the distance as Helena (EVELYNE) and Diana (SUSAN) run through bush in northern Ontario. Diana stops suddenly, gesturing to Helena to be quiet. The drums continue in the distance. They listen for a moment and determine that it's safe.*

EVELYNE:　　*(As Helena.)*
But this exceeding posting day and night,
Must wear your spirits low, we cannot helpe it:
But since you have made the daies and nights as one,
To weare your gentle limbes in my affayres,
Be bold you do so grow in my requitall,
As nothing can unroot you.

Helena offers Diana a small tobacco tie.

I am supposed dead, the fighting over,
My husband hies him home, where spirits aiding,
Wee'll be before our welcome: and the dark.
ALL'S WELL THAT ENDS WELL,
Though time seem so adverse, and means unfit.
We must set free again. Go, go, provide.

Diana exits.

Our remedies oft in ourselves do lye,

EVELYNE stops and begins again in Kanien'kéha.

Sewatié:rens onkwe'shón:'a ionkwanonh-khwa'tsherenhá:wi,
(Our remedies oft in ourselves do lye,)

Nek tsi tiokónte ionkwanonhwerá:tons ne tsi karonhiá:ke né:'e tsi ononhkhwa' shón:'a tehshonkwá:wis
(Which we ascribe to heaven: the fated skye)

Nó:nen kwah nek karonhiá:ke tehshon kwá:wis tsi nahó:ten teionkwatonhon tsó:ni
(Gives us free scope, onely doth backward pull)

> Nek tsi iah te entewakwé:ni toka tsi
> karonhiá:ke tehonaterièn:tare tsi iah te
> wetewahkwísron.
> *(Our slow designes, when we ourselves are dull.)*

> *She exits, following Diana.*

Scene 2

> *The clouds darken in the space, the rain
> threatens. In a field by the edge of the forest.
> Ojibwe reserve. The Clown (SUSAN)
> enters backwards (as some Indigenous
> Contraries would do) followed by Parolles
> (JEAN).*

JEAN: *(As Parolles.)*
I have ere now sir beene better knowne
to you, when I have held familiaritie with
fresher cloathes: but I am now sir muddied in
fortunes mood, and smell somewhat strong
of her strong displeasure.

SUSAN: *(As Clown.)*
Truly, Fortune's displeasure is but sluttish if
it smell so strongly as thou speak'st of: I will
henceforth eat no Fish of Fortune's butt'ring.
Prethee alow the winde.

> *The Clown makes a fanning gesture to
> divert the smell emanating from Parolles.
> SUSAN and JEAN are surprised when the
> wind actually picks up. The sky darkens
> again.*

JEAN: *(As Parolles. Seeing the threat of rain.)*
Nay you neede not to stop your nose sir: I
spake but by a Metaphor.

SUSAN: *(As Clown.)*
Indeed sir, if your Metaphor stinke, I will stop
my nose, or against any mans Metaphor.

The Clown is interrupted by drum sounds.

Riel's comming I know by his Drums. Young man, inquire further after me, I had talke of you last night, though you are a foole and a knave, you shall eate, go too, follow.

JEAN: *(As Parolles.)*
I praise Manitou for you.

They exit.

Scene 3

The Village. Louis Riel (FATHER WILLIAMS) and the Countess (BETH) are honouring Helena's passing to the spirit world.

WILLIAMS: *(As Riel/the King, with French accent.)*
We lost a jewell of her, and our esteeme
Was made much poorer by it.

BETH: *(As the Countess.)*
'Tis past my Chief,
And I beseech your Heart to make it
Naturall rebellion, done i'th blade of youth,
When oyle and fire, too strong for reasons force,
Ore-beares it, and burnes on.

Throughout the following, FATHER WILLIAMS struggles to remember his lines. JEAN feeds them to him.

WILLIAMS: *(As Riel/the King.)*
Our honour'd Mother,
I have forgiven and forgotten all,
Though my revenges were high bent upon him. Well... well... well...

JEAN: Well, call him hither—

WILLIAMS: *(As Riel/the King.)*
                   Well, call him hither; We are...

JEAN: Reconcil'd—

WILLIAMS: *(As Riel/the King.)*
                   We are reconcil'd,

JEAN: And the first view shall kill—

WILLIAMS: *(As Riel/the King.)*
                   And the first view shall *(Fart.)*

> *FATHER WILLIAMS starts to fart*
> *uncontrollably. His final, loudest release*
> *of gas blows the moustache clear off of his*
> *face as he runs off stage. JEAN grabs the*
> *moustache and continues on as Riel, not*
> *missing a beat.*

JEAN: *(As Riel/the King, with French accent.)*
                   All repetition...

> *JEAN removes the moustache and continues*
> *without the accent.*

Let him not aske our pardon,
The nature of his great offence is dead,
And deeper than oblivion, we do burie
Th' incensing reliques of it.

> *Riel stands and gestures for Bertram to*
> *enter. Bertram feels out of place, not sure*
> *if he belongs. The first sound of thunder is*
> *heard in the distance.*

Distracted clouds give way, so stand thou
forth,
The time is faire againe.

> *BETH sings a song her mother taught her*
> *when she was young. She uses a feather to*
> *wipe away Bertram's shame.*

BETH: *(As the Countess, singing in Anishinaabemowin.)*
Gi-maaminonenimaa na gi-maamaa
e-gigiinoo'amaag ozaawegizigewin.
(Remember your mother teaching you hide tanning,)
Maaminonendan debaajimowinan gaa-gii-wiindamaag.
(the stories she told you.)

Gi-maaminonendam ina gi-maamaa
e-zhawenimig zaagibagaawi-giizis.
(Remember your mother's love in May; things growing out from the ground),
Inaabin akiing chi-maaminonendaman
gagina gego gechi-inendaagog.
(Look to the earth to remember all that is important.)

> *Bertram makes a gesture of honour to Riel who notices the pouch.*

JEAN: *(As Riel/the King.)*
Now pray you, let me see that.

> *When asked, Bertram hands Riel the pouch, who examines it and then puts it on.*

This Pouch was mine, and when I gave it Hellen,
I bad her if her fortunes ever stoode
Necessitied to helpe, that by this token
I would releeve her.

JOSEPH: *(As Bertram.)*
How ere it pleases you to take it so,
The pouch was never hers.

BETH: *(As the Countess.)*
Sonne, on my life,
I have seene her weare it, and she reckon'd it
At her lives rate.

JEAN:
>*(As Riel/the King.)*
>If it should prove
>That thou art so inhumane, 'twill not prove so:
>And yet I know not, thou didst hate her deadly,
>And she is dead, which nothing, but to close
>Her eyes my selfe, could win me to beleeve,
>More than to see this Pouch.

SUSAN enters as Diana.

>What woman's that?

SUSAN:
>*(As Diana.)*
>I am in truth a humble Cree
>Derived from ancient ancestors.
>Why do you look so strange upon your wife?

JOSEPH:
>*(As Bertram.)*
>My Chief, this is a fond and desp'rate creature,
>Whom sometime I have laugh'd with.

SUSAN:
>*(As Diana.)*
>O behold this Stone,
>Whose high respect and rich validitie
>Did lack a Paralell: yet for all that
>He gave it to a Commoner a' the Campe
>If I be one.

BETH:
>*(As the Countess.)*
>He blushes, and 'tis hit:
>Of six preceding ancestors that stone
>Confer'd by custom to'th sequent issue
>Hath it beene kept and worn.

JEAN:
>*(As Riel/the King.)*
>She hath that stone of yours.

SUSAN:
>*(As Diana.)*
>I pray you yet,
>(Since you lack vertue, I will lose a husband)
>Send for the Pouch, I will returne it home.

JOSEPH: *(As Bertram.)*
I have it not.

JEAN: *(As Riel/the King.)*
What Pouch was yours I pray you?

SUSAN: *(As Diana.)*
Sir much like
the same upon your chest.

JEAN: *(As Riel/the King.)*
This Pouch was mine, I gave it his first wife.

SUSAN: *(As Diana.)*
The healer that owes the Pouch is sent for,
And she shall surety me. But for this boy,
Who hath abus'd me as he knowes himselfe,
Though yet he never harm'd me, heere I quit
him.
He knowes himselfe my bed he hath defil'd,
And at that time he got his wife with childe:
Dead though she be, she feeles her yong one
kicke:
So there's my riddle, one that's dead is
quicke,
And now behold the meaning.

> *EVELYNE enters as Helena. The drums
> grow.*

JEAN: *(As Riel/the King.)*
Is't reall that I see?

JOSEPH: *(As Bertram.)*
Is't reall that I see?

EVELYNE: *(As Helena, to the King)*
'Tis but the shadow of a wife you see,
The name, and not the thing.

> *The sound of thunder is heard. The students
> look up at the darkening sky with concern.*

(To the Countess.)
O my deere mother do I see you living?
(To Bertram.) When I was like this Maid,
I found you wondrous kinde, there is your Stone,
And looke you, heeres your letter: this it sayes,
When from my hand you can get this Stone, and shew me a childe begotten of thy bodie: that I am father to, then call me husband.
This is done,
Will you be mine now you are doubly wonne?

JOSEPH: *(As Bertram.)*
If she my Chief can make me know this clearly,
Ile love her dearely, ever, ever dearely.

> *The drum swells. JEAN begins to sing a round dance song. Slowly, all the students join in, singing and dancing together. As the song crescendos, the sky releases its pent-up tears and it begins to pour. The students stand in amazement as they hear the sounds of screams and chairs being moved and people scattering.*

Transition 2.12-2.13

> *All of the spirit images appear on the chalkboards.*
>
> *FATHER WILLIAMS tries and fails to erase them.*

Scene 2.13

> *JEAN, JOSEPH, BETH, and SUSAN are all gathered outside the school, everyone with a small bag or suitcase with the exception of BETH. JEAN holds yellow flowers. A beautiful morning light shines.*

JEAN: Really wish we could have been there for your wedding, Susan.

SUSAN: I would have preferred one of you walking me down the aisle instead of Father Williams, but at least he didn't make a speech. Lucas

            and I are meeting him at the gate in five minutes. He's driving us to town.

JOSEPH: Well, that's good, I guess.

SUSAN: Yeah, I guess.

            There's a heavy silence until EVELYNE enters. Her hair is very short.

EVELYNE: *(Extending her medicine pouch.)* I almost forgot this, Miss Ap Dafydd told me I could keep it.

JEAN: I think we did a pretty good job, the five of us. Together.

BETH: Too bad the King and Queen were no-shows.

SUSAN: It's probably for the best that Their Majesties didn't see Father Williams almost poop himself on stage.

JOSEPH: He'd never be hired back for next year if they'd seen *that*.

EVELYNE: Father Williams says he's "not going anywhere anytime soon," so I guess he got lucky.

SUSAN: You really saved the day, Jean.

BETH: It's a miracle Miss Ap Dafydd didn't mention the costumes.

JOSEPH: Or the wigs.

JEAN: She was too busy getting an earful from Principal Clarke about letting us sing those songs.

EVELYNE: Sure would've been nice if she'd taken the fall for me speaking Shakespeare in Kanien'kéha. I knew it wouldn't end well, but I just had to.

JEAN: Doesn't seem fair that you got your head shaved and I got myself a job.

SUSAN: Scruffy head for now, hero forever.

BETH: Still can't believe you agreed to make propaganda films for the government, Jean.

EVELYNE: But being paid, as an actor! An Indian actor!

JEAN: I *hope* they actually pay me. It's a new company called The National Film Board of Canada—what a name. They thought my Louis Riel was "deeply compelling." I'm hoping this'll lead me to some big-time movies. They told me I just need to learn how to ride a horse.

JOSEPH: What about you, Evelyne? How did it work out with your father?

EVELYNE: He actually likes the idea of me becoming an army nurse, even if it means losing my status. I'm going to slip in our traditional medicines when no one's looking and make sure I'm there for all those soldiers that Jean's going to encourage to enlist!

JEAN: Yeah, sorry about that.

JOSEPH: *(To EVELYNE.)* If you ever want to visit the bush in northern Ontario, you know where to find me. *(Beat.)* I can't believe I'm actually going home.

BETH: A lot can change in seven years.

JEAN: *(Giving BETH a flower.)* You'll be out of here in no time too, Beth.

EVELYNE: And you have *Twelfth Night* to look forward to.

BETH: Father Williams is directing *HMS Pinafore* next year. Goodbye, then.

             JEAN, EVELYNE, and SUSAN exit. BETH turns to go trying to hide her tears.

JOSEPH: Beth, wait.

             JOSEPH gives BETH a long hug.

             Ni-maamaanaan *(our Mother)* is going to be real proud of you when I tell her you sang her song.

             He turns to go but struggles to leave.

             Gi-zhawenimin *(I love you).*

BETH: Gi-zhawenimin *(I love you).*

             We hear the sounds of a large group of children singing as JOSEPH finally pulls himself away and exits, leaving BETH by herself watching him go. She starts to run after him, but stops herself.

             In days of yore, from Britain's shore,
             Came the white men to our land,
             They put us in these wretched schools
             On promise of better days
             Must kill the savage, save the child
             The future's now or never
             But all we've learned is how to sing
             The Maple Leaf forever!

BETH's tears begin to fall as she joins in singing the chorus, a pasted smile on her face, as the lights fade to black.

The Maple Leaf, our emblem dear,
The Maple Leaf forever!
God save our King and Heaven bless
The Maple Leaf forever!

The End

Afterword

The following interview was published in Canadian Theatre Review, *Volume 197, Winter 2024. It is reprinted here with the generous permission of* CTR.

"1939" Reflections on Adaptation, Indigenous Theàtre, and Shakespeare's Legacy: An interview with Jani Lauzon and Kaitlyn Riordan

Interviewer: Sorouja Moll

At a creative juncture during the 2020 writing process of the play *1939,* and then again after the 2022 World Premiere at the Stratford Festival, I interviewed playwrights Jani Lauzon and Kaitlyn Riordan. I asked Lauzon and Riordan to share their insights about the development of the work and the challenges they faced when collaboratively devising an adaptation of Shakespeare set in a residential school in early twentieth-century Canada.

1) What was the impulse that brought you two together to examine Shakespeare and colonial histories in Canada?

Lauzon: Kaitlyn approached me about the possibility of directing for Shakespeare in the Ruff at some point. We spent our first meeting talking about our love of Shakespeare and I shared with Kaitlyn my introduction and then subsequent struggle with finding opportunities to perform. I also shared with her the discoveries I had made with finding myself inside the work and how I had developed a pedagogy for teaching Shakespeare to Indigenous students at The Centre for Indigenous Theatre. Being the amazing woman that she is, she saw the potential for an interesting play and reached out to see if I would be interested in writing it with her. Everything about our first meeting was easy. She is open and generous and passionate and all of that helped to shape our working relationship moving forward. She was also more on top of reaching out to others that could potentially support us financially as we explored what it would mean to write a play like this. Not sure we would be here without her initial push.

Riordan: It began with our mutual love of Shakespeare and desire to centre Indigenous voices in his works. Understanding my inherent privilege, as a white settler here on Turtle Island, is an ongoing process. One of the steps on this journey has been meeting Jani, learning from her generosity, and understanding our two different experiences performing Shakespeare in our careers. We both love it, especially performing it outdoors. We connect to the poetry, the rhythms, the structure, the vulnerabilities, the passions, and on and on. As a white woman of European descent, my place in a Shakespearean play was never questioned; through Jani's sharing, I learned that her experience has been different.

When I lived in the UK, I often struggled with "imposter" syndrome being from "the colonies." I feared I would never know Shakespeare the way the English did, and used their accent when performing him in England. It never even occurred to me to use my own voice. But why? I have often felt that I couldn't bring Shakespeare to me, I had to go to him. Jani's stories and the resonance she spoke about between traditional Indigenous storytelling and the way Shakespeare used language got me wondering about his legacy in this country; one apart from his place of birth and rooted on this land. I realized that we all live under the shadow of colonization, some much more than others, but that our mindset is so deeply influenced by it. So if Shakespeare is universal, which I believe many of his themes are, how do we authentically bring him to us, here, in Canada? That question, combined with the shutting out of Indigenous voices in Shakespeare, and a desire to make better known the history of residential schools, led us to this play.

2) As part of the play's development the working title *1939: All's Well That Ends Well*, the play within the play was used. Why was this chosen?

Lauzon: Both Kaitlyn and I brought forward ideas for plays. What I liked about *All's Well That Ends Well* was how some of the core themes and the circumstances of the characters could be translated into an Indigenous experience to a broader degree than the others we contemplated. Not everything fits, of course, which would be the case with any of his plays, but there were so many similarities. The added bonus came later with the themes of war and monarchy when we decided to set our play in 1939. Our work as playwrights is to dig deeper into the text to really examine those intersections. But Shakespeare makes it easy as the beauty in the writing is based so firmly in relationships and human experience. Racism, class structure, war, hierarchy, love (or lack of it), humour; these are universal experiences.

Riordan: Ultimately, it really resonated with the themes we wanted to explore, and like all of Shakespeare's comedies, there's so much angst, suffering, and loneliness just beneath the surface. Also, people don't know that play as well as some of his others, and that allowed us more freedom to play.

3) In a 2018 email, Kaitlyn noted that you both had "narrowed in on a moment in history" for the setting of the play: 1939, and the King's visit to Canada. What compelled you to identify this date in history?

Lauzon: Ahhh…my recollection of this may be different from Kaitlyn's, but what I recall is that we were looking for a dramatic framework that would justify the resources and effort put into a production of a Shakespeare play at an otherwise cash-strapped residential school. The promise of a royal visit and the need to impress them with something extraordinary gave us a good dramaturgical container. It turned out to be a perfect time in so many ways. The numbers of students at the schools had grown substantially, the effects of the schools were already being analyzed and white civilization had laid the stronghold on what was considered Canadian identity. All this helped to create a container for the story that we were interested in telling.

Riordan: I think I was watching a lot of *The Crown* at the time... But truly, I am amazed by how obsessed we are with the monarchy here in Canada; we have bought into the fairy tale, despite the fact that to me, the monarchy represents the epitome of colonization. But extraordinary moments, like the first visit of a sitting King and Queen, also allows for extraordinary things to happen. The stakes are high, and the theatre that I'm most interested in has very high stakes. The late '30s also represented the height of the residential school system and a world on the verge of another world war: the stakes couldn't be higher.

4) During the second workshop (January 2020; Toronto, Ontario), you asked the actors to respond to a series of questions and among them was the query "Whose story is it?" How would you respond to this question?

Lauzon: I always hoped that it would be the students' story, as a group. But western dramaturgy suggests that it should be one person's story. The question was asked because we are interested in challenging the western structure and to see what was resonating for the actors who joined us in the workshop. I love working with actors. They are smart and intuitive. If it's the students' story, then they discover together that they can take agency which is only possible to do as a group. The opposite to divide and conquer. The students experience and recognize their resilience together, to the betterment of their individual journeys. We have succeeded, I think, although with each new draft we have to re-examine that concept. There are so many points of view and so many wonderful characters that we are falling in love with, that the trick is to keep it firmly rooted in the POV of the students and to ensure that the spirit of the story is honoured with whatever structure and central through line that it leads us to in the end.

Riordan: The reason we asked this question is that Jani and I have always stressed that this story must belong to the Indigenous students in this play or we would not be honouring Survivors of residential schools in the way that we aim to. It's a question we ask of ourselves and come back to a lot.

5) In the summer of 2019, we travelled to Algoma University in Sault Ste. Marie to visit the Shingwauk Residential Schools Centre's archive and meet with the director, Elizabeth Edgar Webkamigad and researcher/curator Krista McCracken. What did you discover in the archives at the former residential school?

Lauzon: The most important thing for me was to connect with the wit, the humour, the intelligence, the anger, and the resilience of the students. Reading their stories, even though we knew they had been curated, was heartbreaking but rewarding. Their voices. Their words.

The other important aspect of that trip for me was meeting Elder Shirley Horn. Not only for the research we were doing for the play but just in general. I think of her often when I am about to complain about something or feel despondent. I like to think that some of our characters grew up to be like Shirley. She is resilience in action. What she has accomplished, what she inspires in others despite the horrific experience she went through is the perfect example of how strong Indigenous People are. The archive is an invaluable resource, and of course the people running it are incredibly helpful. We could have easily spent weeks there.

Riordan: Ironically, I think one of the things that became most clear to me was how the history of this atrocity has been buried. There were so many times when what we gleaned from the materials at the archive was either what (or who) was left out or what we could read between the lines. Thankfully, because of the courage of Survivors, we now have many of their stories published and on public record, but it became very clear that this part of our history was never meant to be preserved. Seeing the work being done at the archive and at Algoma University to preserve the history of the building and honour the Survivors we met there was very inspiring and a living, breathing example to be emulated. While we were there, we also got to meet with the Chancellor of the University, Elder Shirley Horn. Shirley is a survivor of Shingwauk Residential School and has been a huge part of bringing together fellow Survivors, who now advise the University on every major decision they make. Shirley is a force to be reckoned with and brings a profound generosity to her work.

6) During this research trip we also visited the ruins of two residential schools: one in Spanish, Ontario and one in Wikwemikong on Manitoulin Island. What are your reflections about this experience and how did this knowledge impact the play's development?

Lauzon: The school in Spanish had the most impact on me. While I understand that it's on private land and it's impossible for a family to financially take on the responsibility of preserving its legacy, my heart broke to realize that the government had absolutely no interest in bringing light to that history. Those ruins should be made into a heritage site. The ruins in Wikwemikong have caretakers from the community and the site is used in a positive way to incorporate storytelling and theatre performance that help to reclaim the space, its history. But in Spanish, the physical building represents the continued and crumbling relationship of that history with the average Canadian and our government.

Riordan: My experience visiting these sites reinforced what I expressed above; as a country, we've had no interest in preserving the history of residential schools. Not only that, but we have also not taken ownership of that history and accepted it as truth. The condition of these sites, with a lack of information and sometimes on private property, did not make them very accessible, much like the history itself. However, knowing some of the stories from these actual buildings, and understanding some of the implications for so many people of what happened in those buildings, visiting the sites was profound. Having read Basil H. Johnston's book, *Indian School Days*, about having gone to Spanish, I was flooded with images he had described, and classmates he had had. The land itself had witnessed so much suffering and walking on it myself, I was very humbled. I think, as humans, we naturally put ourselves in other people's shoes; as a playwright and actor, I also do it professionally. I couldn't help but imagining my six-year-old self arriving at this place and wondering how I would have managed the fear and cruelty that awaited me. The experience in the archives, meeting Shirley, and visiting these sites deepened my resolve to honour the Survivors with as much truth and humanity as possible.

7) Audre Lorde (1984, 2007) explains that "the master's tools will never dismantle the master's house. They may allow us to temporarily beat him at his game, but will never bring about genuine change" (2007, 112). As the actors explore and rupture the "tools" of the "house" and make visible the hegemony using an adaptation of a Shakespearean play at a residential school, how is Lorde's sense of futility in the dismantling of the house challenged? Moreover, was there a specific time when the actors' work and your writing began to shift toward Lorde's fuller explanation of her statement: "this fact is only threatening to those [...] who still define the master's house as their only source of support" and "It is learning how to take our differences and make them strengths"? (2007, 112). Or, how did the play's development seek to empower and ignite individual and collective agency?

Lauzon: That could be a whole thesis in itself! I know that I am not directly answering your question but feel compelled to mention that what I appreciate in Lorde's essay is her observation that "Divide and conquer, in our world, must become define and empower." What should have been given to those students, to all First Nations, Métis and Inuit children was empowerment. But the master's house couldn't allow that, because a shift in the assumption of superiority would have been necessary. But in our play, although the students are not successful in their efforts to "dismantle the master's house," they are successful in empowering themselves. That was always our goal. We wanted to show the incredible resilience that is inherent in Indigenous spirit. The fact that the students gain some agency is a small step in comparison to the larger need of burning the house down, but large in the sense of the building of a new house, one brick at a time, for future generations. Returning to Shirley Horn, the work that she does now, important work on reconciliation and empowerment, was made possible because of her experience at residential school. She speaks to having had to go through what she went through to fulfill her purpose now. We are rebuilding the house now as a result of the sacrifice those students went through earlier. It has taken this long. It will take longer, but it's happening. We can't anticipate how long it will take to dismantle the master's house. In our play, the master's house cannot be dismantled. That is the tragedy of it. Beth, the only student returning to the school the following year, will be forced to return to Miss Ap Dafydd's comfort and understanding of how Shakespeare "should" be done. Any glimmer of permanent change will be overshadowed by the tools of the master to reconstruct his house. But in our play is also the glimmer of hope. The power of the Seven Generation teachings, that what we do will affect those who are seven generations ahead of us. The actions of those students, I like to think, had that effect on today's generation and the fact that the master's house is finally being transformed, albeit still not as fast as it could be, as resistance, it is very powerful.

Riordan: Lorde's quote is one I think about a lot these days. In the case of *1939*, it comes back to self-expression for me. The frustrating truth is that we know these students don't dismantle "the master's house," but what is it that they do achieve? For me, performing Shakespeare has been a form of self-expression that I have never experienced elsewhere. The emotional depth of the language, the rhythms, the structure are like no other I have encountered and help me to reveal part of myself when I speak it. Jani and I asked ourselves; "How would our students get to that point?", which we have both identified as experiences we've shared. We knew it wasn't in the way that the teachers wanted it done, it had to be something the students discovered for themselves. Knowing that Shakespeare holds that possibility of self-expression, like so much great art, we had to figure out how they would get there and then how they'd get away with it, which is a whole other thing when you're trapped inside of an oppressive regime.

8) During the January 2020 workshop, Shakespeare's *All's Well* transforms into an "Indian Shakespeare." When considering your experiences with adaptation as a process, what was the prompt, in this case, that pushed the Shakespearean text into an adaptation? Why is this possible with Shakespeare?

Lauzon: I have spent many years contemplating adaptation. I have not been able to definitively answer why I am drawn to Shakespeare, specifically. But I do know that, in general, it is the structure of the language in comparison to Indigenous language: the similarity in the use of metaphor or description as well as the rhythm. There is also a big connection in the relationship of spirit (or gods) to human condition and the power of the natural world. What really struck me about the possible adaptation for ACT V in *All's Well That Ends Well* is the ceremonial aspect of the reuniting of community, spirit, love, the return from war and the healing that community brings to fracture. From my humble perspective, this is possible because all of Shakespeare's broader themes encompass these universal human circumstances. Those themes could be applied to any culture. For our goals with 1939, the recognition that the reuniting of community would be surrounded in ceremony remains our focus and why we are able to contextualize it as an "Indian Shakespeare." We are layering that worldview into the events of the reunion and the importance of responsibility to community in our ACT V.

Riordan: Jani and I both have a lot of experience with Shakespearean adaptations, so I believe we were naturally drawn to that way forward. (I like to think I've come a long way since performing Viola with an English accent back in 2005). Jani has also been asked to "Indigenize" Shakespeare a lot lately, and those requests have shaped our desire to explore that with all of its complications and complexities. "Is it even possible?" is an ongoing question.

9) At the second workshop (January 2020, Toronto, Ontario), during one of the physical exercises that focused on the Shakespearean text, one line in particular affected all the actors and generated lengthy and extemporaneous rounds of communal repetition. The King's line "Is't real that I see?" (5.3.305) greets a returning Helena, who was thought dead. She enters the scene to meet the grieving cast. Why do you think this line resonated with the actors?

Lauzon: Ah, each actor is so individual and I can't speak to what their personal connection is, but for me it is deeply rooted in metaphor. For the students in the play, that moment is not only a return to the community they have been torn from but a reuniting with those they thought were dead to them, or at the very least lost to them. It is also an opportunity to examine what we think is real; what we were forced to believe vs. the truth of who we are. The students at those schools struggled to remain connected to their identity, what they had been taught. They were subject to a powerful hypnosis. They realize, as characters in the play, through Shakespeare's words, that they have the ability to perceive their experience based on what their gut is telling them.

Riordan: As modern actors, with much of our texts rooted in realism, it can be challenging to go on the ride of the final moments in many of Shakespeare's comedies. He takes us to a place of awe and wonder, which often invites us (as the performers, not just the audience) to suspend our disbelief and exist in a space where anything is possible; people coming back from the dead, Jupiter descending on the back of an Eagle, statues coming to life. As a director, one of Jani's many strengths is to equip actors to go on the journey of the text. In that workshop, I witnessed actors give themselves over to the wonder that Shakespeare beckons us to.

10) As you moved the playwriting forward, what was the greatest challenge you and the actors faced when developing a play set in a residential school with the use of Shakespeare as a creative vehicle? What do you hope is learned from this experience and the play?

Lauzon: Two things weigh on my heart. The first is to never undermine the severe and brutal circumstances that those students faced. We are writing a play with humour, but it doesn't mean that our intention is to make light of the situations and the soul-cracking experiences that each and every one of those students went through. We hope to honour them by shedding light on their resilience, their brilliance, their talent and their ability to survive an otherwise impossible situation. The other challenge of course is "Why Shakespeare?" Why use the words of the dead white guy? It is not our intention to negate or disregard the incredible First Nations, Métis and Inuit writers that are extremely talented. Instead, we wanted to address the fact that both Kaitlyn and I not only share a deep passion for his work but that Shakespeare's plays have resonated with generation after generation all over the world because of the craft, the universality of the themes, and that so much about the action of his plays is routed in universal relationship. We can find ourselves in those relationships no matter who we are and where we come from. The wars may be different, the kings and queens maybe look different, be dressed differently, the lovers may have different names but the reasons they fall in love and the journey to realize that love is the same. We also wanted to explore the way in which Shakespeare's text was used to build the colonial house we call Canada. Shakespeare was taught in every colonized school around the world in order to teach British politics, history and its legal system. To a lesser degree this included the "Indian" students at the church and government-run residential schools. This was not only done overtly in curriculum but also through the use of language in the media and propaganda of the day. Art can be a powerful tool used far beyond the playwright's original intentions. In Shakespeare's case, his work was used to help build an empire and bring down so many others. Can't imagine he would be too pleased to know that. In my heart I am sure that was not his intention.

Riordan: The challenge of using Shakespeare for self-expression, with Indigenous students, while not making him a "white saviour," is real. The students in this play are their own "saviours"; they advocate, negotiate, and fight for their own truth to be front and centre. They support each other and find strength in numbers and do so within the confines of a residential school in 1939. The boundaries are undeniable in that setting, so they use what they are given: Shakespeare. Within that form, they find freedom and self-expression, both because he is a great writer and because they are deeply intelligent and determined.

Another challenge is that this play includes humour. Jani and I both believe that humour can be a very effective way to speak about difficult truths. "Play the opposite," an acting coach once told me; it's what we do in real life. As I've mentioned, honouring Survivors is at the core of our intentions with writing this play; using humour to do that may not seem like the most obvious path forward, but we want to celebrate their resilience, and laughter is a profound source of resilience.

Epilogue

11). The world premiere of *1939* opened September 11, 2022 at the Stratford Festival. While I am certain there are many aspects of the play that remain profoundly memorable, after seeing the production and upon reflection, what moment continues to resonate with you? And as the second part of this question: What would you like future audiences to learn from the play?

Riordan: Elder Elizabeth Stevens shared with us, very early in the process, that language is culture. She is an advocate and teacher of Anishinaabemowin and helped us understand the ways in which language reflects a cultural perspective beyond words. One of the students in the play, Evelyne, grew up speaking Kanien'kéha and decides, in an act of rebellion that will have consequences, to speak some of the Shakespearean text in her own language during the final performance. Watching the performer, Wahsonti:io Kirby, who also grew up speaking Kanien'kéha, speak that language in front of an audience for the first time was profound. The layers upon layers of resonance were felt by the audience as they leaned in, rooting for Evelyne with every atom of their being.

I don't know that my ambition for an audience is to learn so much as it is for them to feel, to question, to empathize, to ask questions, to provoke conversation. I believe the theatre offers a space where nuance and contradiction can exist, which is at the heart of the human experience and my hope for all audiences.

Lauzon: The students in our play sing a round dance song on stage at the Studio Theatre. For me, that was profound and to my knowledge the first time in the festival's history that has happened. Those melodies, the drum, they reverberated through the building, inviting ancestors to join them dancing and singing on a spot that very well may have been a place where a round dance had taken place many years before. In some ways it's about reclaiming space. In other ways it's a celebration of the resilience we propose in our play, manifesting years later with five well-trained, exceptional Indigenous actors on stage at one of the world's renowned theatre festivals. What I know to be true is that the play profoundly moved audience members, challenged others, brought some to tears, blew some minds and opened hearts. My hope is we can continue to make that happen.

NOTES

Shirley Horn is an Elder and Chief in her community, the Missanabie Cree First Nation, and a residential school Survivor who served as the first Chancellor of Algoma University (2015-2021). Horn is a founder of the Children of Shingwauk Alumni Association (CSAA), a member of the Missanabie Cree Elders' Council, Co-Founder of the Echoes of the World Drum Festival, a former member of the Shingwauk Education Trust (SET), and an accomplished article.

WORK CITED

Lorde, Audre. "The Master's Tools Will Never Dismantle the Master's House." 1984. *Sister Outsider: Essays and Speeches.* Ed. Berkeley, CA: Crossing Press. 110–114. 2007. Print.

1939 Study Guide

The study guide created for the 2022 Stratford Festival production of 1939 *is excerpted here by permission of the Stratford Festival and the guide's creators and contributors: Dr. Sorouja Moll, Robin Jones-Stadelbauer, Elder Jean Becker, and Elder Liz Stevens, as well as Arielle Zamora and the Education Department at the Stratford Festival. Biographies of the guide's creators and contributors can be found at the end of the guide.*

The 1939 *study guide launched an initiative led jointly by the University of Waterloo's Office of Indigenous Relations and Faculty of Arts alongside the Stratford Festival to promote deeper engagement with Indigenous artists, artistry, and productions across institutions.*

Born of both family legacy and the Calls to Action of the Truth and Reconciliation Commission, *1939* has been guided by Indigenous Elders, Survivors and ceremony throughout its development.

SYNOPSIS

At a Residential School in northern Ontario, five students are ordered to gather in a classroom. Two of them, Joseph Summers and his sister, Beth, have been at the school for seven years, but its policy of separating siblings has largely kept them apart—until now. Susan Blackbird, an orphan who has been there since she was four, struggles to connect with her barely remembered Cree heritage, while newcomer Evelyne Rice tries to avoid punishment by repressing her Mohawk culture and language. Jean Delorme, as a Métis student, is a rarity at the school and struggles to fit in.

English teacher Sian Ap Dafydd explains the reason for their summons: they have been chosen to entertain King George VI and his Queen on their forthcoming visit with a student performance of Shakespeare's *All's Well That Ends Well*. Firmly colonial in her notions and intentions, Ap Dafydd is as determined to get her young actors to deliver the "big round vowels" she considers essential to speaking Shakespeare as she is to show the royal couple how the students are learning to be "good little Canadians."

But as rehearsals proceed, the students' agency erupts as they learn about each other and discover parallels between the play's characters and their own experiences. Confronting individual and collective tragedy with humour and strength, the students undertake a journey of self-discovery and empowerment—their resilience evoking Helena's line in *All's Well*: "Our remedies oft in ourselves do lie."

GRADE RECOMMENDATION

7+

CURRICULUM CONNECTIONS

- Global Competencies
    - ∞ Collaboration, Communication, Critical Thinking, Creativity, Learning to Learn/Self-Awareness

- Grades 7-8
    - ∞ Indigenous Languages
    - ∞ The Arts
    - ∞ Social Studies
    - ∞ Language
    - ∞ Health and Physical Education

- Grades 9-12
    - ∞ First Nations, Métis and Inuit Studies
    - ∞ Indigenous Languages
    - ∞ The Arts

- ∞ Canadian and World Studies
- ∞ English
- ∞ Health and Physical Education
- Grades 11-12
  - ∞ Social Sciences and Humanities
- Post-Secondary
  - ∞ Suitable for courses in disciplines such as Indigenous Studies, Arts, Canadian Studies, Cultural Studies, Drama, English, Fine Arts, History, Human Rights, Religious Studies, Social Development Studies, Teacher Education, and Theatre.

THEMES

- The Art of Resilience
- Collective Agency and First Nations, Métis and Inuit Activism
- Colonialism and the War on Indigenous Peoples
- The Doctrine of Discovery
- Indigeneity and Gender
- Giving Voice to Missing and Murdered Indigenous Children
- The Influence of the Written Word in Media and from Government
- Language as Culture, Language as Identity, Language as Power
- Loneliness and Isolation
- The Power of Storytelling and Theatre
- Residential Schools
- The Role of Humour in Navigating Racism, Trauma and Systemic Oppression
- Shakespeare and Adaptation, Disrupting the Myth That There is a "Right Way" to Perform Shakespeare

- Truth and Reconciliation
- 1939: History and Significance

DISCUSSION AND REFLECTION QUESTIONS BEFORE READING THE PLAY

- What is colonialism? How does Shakespeare represent colonialism? Why does it become both important and challenging for the students in the play to disrupt/ decolonize the colonial models of Shakespeare? What happens when they do?

- What are Residential and Day Schools? What are their connections with colonialism? When considering your experience at school, what do you see as being different from a Residential or Day School?

- How does the media influence your beliefs about communities other than your own? What can you do to ensure you are mindful of the media you take in?

- There are more than 630 First Nation communities in Canada, which represent more than 50 Nations and 50 Indigenous languages. Many Inuit live in 53 communities across the northern regions comprising Inuvialuit (Northwest Territories and Yukon), Nunavik (Northern Quebec), Nunatsiavut (Labrador), and Nunavut as well as in communities across Canada. With a unique history, culture, language, and territory, Métis are a distinct Indigenous people living across Canada. When learning about Indigeneity, why do you think specificity is important?

Educator Resource: Indigenous Peoples and Communities
https://www.rcaanc-cirnac.gc.ca/eng/1100100013785/1529102490303

QUESTIONS AFTER READING THE PLAY

- What particular part of the play stands out in your mind—a line, an action, a theme, or something else? Why do you think this resonates for you?

- Did anything surprise you or resonate with you about Indigenous Knowledges shared within the play? Share three pieces of Indigenous knowledge that you remember.

- Do you see parallels between how the Indigenous children in *1939* were perceived and treated at the school and how Indigenous people are perceived in Canada today? If yes, were these perceptions negative or positive? How do you think these perceptions are perpetuated?

- Identify one behaviour, rule, or restriction placed on an Indian* Residential School attendee and how this behaviour, rule or restriction could potentially impact the attendee for the remainder of their life and potentially their children and grandchildren's lives.

FURTHER QUESTIONS

- Why is acknowledging the specific Indigenous territories in which you live, work, and play important? Using the Native Land Digital map (https://native-land.ca), locate the territory or territories you live on, as well as the Languages and Treaties.

- In *1939*, where and how do racism and discrimination appear? Share examples of how racism and discrimination are still active in Canada today.

- Identify the connections between the characters in *1939* and the territories they are from, as well as their ancestral homes. How might learning more about these connections advance your understanding of the characters in the play? If the characters do not know where they are from, how might this affect their experience of themselves and their interpersonal relationships?

- Define "resilience." What does resilience mean to you? Think about a time when you were resilient. In what ways do you recognize resilience in the young people in the play? Which specific scene or character stands out to you?

- Read and listen to the CBC report titled "Stories of Mohawk Institute Residential School…" What does it look and feel like to remember and honour Survivors of the Residential and Day School systems today? Think of three actions you will take to do so in your own life.

- How did the elements of humour in 1939 impact your experience? What effect do the combined genres of comedy and tragedy have on the play? What role do you think humour plays in exploring issues of racism and discrimination?

- Why do you think the playwrights included "The Maple Leaf Forever"? What is its significance to the story?

- In what ways does 1939 respond to the 83rd Call to Action from the Truth and Reconciliation Commission? Why might it be important for Indigenous and non-Indigenous artists to work together on projects that contribute to rebuilding relationships among non-Indigenous and Indigenous people, communities and Nations? What might this approach be missing?

- What did watching the students experiencing cultural authenticity in juxtaposition with inauthenticity reveal to you? Authenticity: traditional medicines, rituals, sharing of Indigenous Knowledges, individual characters' differentiating perspectives. Inauthenticity: costumes, stereotypes, generalizations.

  Extension: How might this reflect contemporary issues of cultural appropriation vs. cultural appreciation? List three examples found in media sources.

- Reflect on your cultural heritage(s). Then, think about a culture that you have experienced (i.e. through language, nationality, rituals, holidays, food, etc.) that you are not familiar with. How do you begin to respectfully engage with cultures that are unfamiliar to yours and have conversations? What are the challenges? Suggest three ways in which we could begin to work through these challenges.

- Define "reconciliation." Define "conciliation." How are these two actions different? Why might one be more effective than the other?

Educator Resource: *Imaginary Spaces of Conciliation and Reconciliation* by David Garneau (2012)

*Note: The term "Indian" when used to describe First Nations people is derogatory and offensive. This language is used in this Study Guide as it was and is still used by the government of Canada within its legislation (Atlohsa).

MINDS ON: BEFORE READING THE PLAY

Exercise: *Residential Schools in Canada: A Timeline*

Objective: To reflect on current knowledge and build understanding of the Residential School system in what is now called Canada. To respond to the historical and present-day contexts of First Nations, Métis and Inuit resilience in the process of decolonization.

Materials: Video by Heritage Canada, access to the internet, monitor and speakers for presentation, writing utensils and paper.

1. Invite students to jot down their current knowledge of the Residential School system. If known, write where they learned what they know.

2. Watch the YouTube video Residential Schools in Canada: A Timeline https://www.youtube.com/watch?v=VFgNI1lfe0A

3. Split class into groups to complete shared research.

   a. Define "assimilation." Why was this an objective for the governing bodies of Residential Schools?

   b. Who is Dr. Peter Bryce? Why is he important in our understanding of the legacies of Residential Schools?

   c. What is the Indian Act? What are its implications for Indigenous Peoples in Canada?

   d. What is the "Sixties Scoop"? How does it continue to have implications for Indigenous Peoples today?

   e. Who is Phil Fontaine? What was his role in creating change in government policy?

   f. Who is Justice Murray Sinclair? What is the important statement featured in the video that he made in reference to the reconciliation process? Share three examples of what has been done in the past year that demonstrates active remembrance.

POSSIBLE EXTENSIONS

Exploring Apologies

- What makes a meaningful apology?

- Review former prime minister Stephen Harper's Statement of apology to former students of Indian Residential Schools in 2008.

- What do you see as potential issues with this apology? What would you change in this apology?

Educator Resource: Harper, P.M. Stephen. Statement of apology to former students of Indian Residential Schools. [Ottawa]: Government of Canada. Web. 11 Jun. 2008. https://www.rcaanc-cirnac.gc.ca/eng/1100100015644/1571589171655

The Meaning of Intergenerational

- Ask students to define "intergenerational." Before your students attend the show, invite them to be mindful of the intergenerational experiences within the characters' lives. Have them write down one example that stands out to them.

MINDS ON: AFTER READING THE PLAY

Exercise: *Responding to Rehearsal*

Objective: To listen and respond to a conversation between community Elders and the play's director as they respond to their experience attending a rehearsal of *1939*.

Materials: Video found at: https://vimeo.com/766085886/ 10e8dc9e9a, speaker and monitor, device with internet access, paper and writing materials.

In the video, you will meet:

- ∞ Elder Elizabeth (Liz) Stevens of Ojibwe and Potawatomi lineage, residing in Kettle & Stony Point First Nation. Liz is an Ojibwe Language Instructor, Consulting Elder at the Stratford Festival and a Script Consultant on *1939*.

- ∞ Elder Jean Becker, who is Inuk, a member of the Nunatsiavut Territory of Labrador and Associate Vice-President of the Office of Indigenous Relations at the University of Waterloo.

- ∞ Jani Lauzon, a multidisciplinary artist of Métis/ French/Finnish ancestry. Jani is the co-playwright and director of *1939*.

1. Watch the conversation as a class.

2. On their own, students write down one takeaway and something that surprised them during the conversation.

3. In small groups, discuss these takeaways and discoveries.

Exercise: 1939 in The News

Objective: To explore a primary source from the year 1939 and interrogate the representation of events in the media.

Materials: Copies of the article, pieces of butcher paper with a large print copy of the article secured in the centre (one per group), markers and highlighters.

1. Read the 1939 coverage of the Royal Tour in the *Ottawa Citizen* (pp. 1–3).

2. In small groups, students gather around a piece of butcher paper with the article in the centre.

3. Pose the question: "Who is represented in the article?" Students use their markers to call attention to who is mentioned in the article—in silence.

4. Pose the question: "What might be missing from the article?" Ask students to add and write down questions they have about what could be absent from the article—in silence.

5. Ask students to reflect on their experience of reading *1939*.

6. Pose the question: "How do the students and the figure of Madge Macbeth (the reporter) attempt to change this narrative? Why might this be important?" Ask students to discuss, using examples from *1939*.

Educator Resource: *Ottawa Citizen* (May 19, 1939). pp. 1–3 can be accessed here: https://news.google.com/newspapers?id= QI0vAAAAIBAJ&sjid=6tsFAAAAIBAJ&pg=6971%2C1942633

Connection to the Archives: Shingwauk Residential Schools Centre

The Shingwauk Residential Schools Centre (SRSC) is a cross-cultural research and educational project of Algoma University (through the technological and archival expertise of the Arthur A. Wishart Library) and the Children of Shingwauk Alumni Association (CSAA), which includes former students of the Residential Schools, staff, descendants, family, and friends. Algoma University is located on the site (and uses some of the buildings) of the former Shingwauk and Wawanosh Indian Residential Schools in Sault Ste. Marie. Governance for the SRSC runs through a joint AU/CSAA Heritage Committee, which shares responsibility for the Centre evenly between the two partners.

Krista McCracken, Researcher/Curator and their team offered research tools, archival documents, and resource links which supported the development of 1939. Jani Lauzon, Kaitlyn Riordan and Dr. Sorouja Moll visited the SRSC to explore the archives, meet with Shirley Horn, first Chancellor of Algoma University and Survivor, the Children of Shingwauk Alumni Association, as well as artists and community members. Explore the public archive and contact the Centre for more information. http://archives.algomau.ca/main/?q=node/28470

The Mush Hole Project (2016, 2022)

The original Mush Hole Project was presented in 2016 and was an immersive, site-specific art and performance installation at the former Mohawk Institute Indian Residential School (Woodland Cultural Centre) in Brantford. This collaborative project aimed to respond to the Truth and Reconciliation Commission of Canada's Calls to Action and to preserve, query, and reveal the complex personal, political, and public narratives around Canada's Residential School system.

The objective of the Mush Hole Project (http://www. mushholeproject.ca/#mush-hole) was to engage with the site of Canada's first Residential School as a space in which Indigenous and non-Indigenous artists and scholars can meet and 1) acknowledge the Residential School legacy, 2) challenge the concepts of "truth" and "reconciliation," and 3) practise interdisciplinary art and performative methods of decolonization.

Dejidwaya'do:weht *(We are Thinking of it Again)*: Mush Hole 2.0 aimed to raise the public profile of Residential Schools and their ongoing devastating impact through a cross-cultural artistic lens that was showcased digitally as a three-day virtual stream. This project was funded through the Canada Council for the Arts' Digital Now Fund.

Installation in Mush Hole 2.0 by Three Collective. To access the stream of Dejidwaya'do:weht *(We are Thinking of it Again)*, contact the Woodland Cultural Centre at https:// woodlandculturalcentre.ca

About the Authors of the Study Guide

Elder Jean Becker

University of Waterloo, Associate Vice-President, Office of Indigenous Relations

Jean is Inuk and a member of the Nunatsiavut Territory of Labrador. As the Associate Vice-President of Indigenous Relations, Jean provides strategic leadership to articulate the University of Waterloo–specific response to the Truth and Reconciliation Calls to Action and identifies systemic and systematic changes that move beyond the Calls to Action by creating a long-term vision of decolonization and indigenization for the university.

Elder Liz (Elizabeth) Stevens

Script Consultant for *1939*

Liz Stevens is of Ojibwe and Potawatomi lineage residing in Kettle & Stony Point First Nation. She is an Ojibwe Language Instructor in her community and the Consulting Elder at the Stratford Festival.

Robin Jones-Stadelbauer

University of Waterloo, Associate Director, Office of Indigenous Relations

Robin is Anishinaabe from Neyaashiinigmiing (Chippewas of Nawash Unceded First Nation) and has a long history at Waterloo. As the Associate Director, Robin supports the

Associate Vice-President Indigenous Relations in their strategic vision and leadership, represents the AVP, takes leadership on key projects, and is responsible for the daily operations of the Indigenous Relations Office.

Dr. Sorouja Moll

Research Dramaturge (2018–2022) for *1939*

Lecturer, University of Waterloo, Department of Communication Arts

Sorouja Moll has a PhD in Humanities and Interdisciplinary Studies (Concordia) specializing in the fields of Communication, English, and Art History. She also holds a BA and MA in English from the University of Guelph, School of English and Theatre. As an interdisciplinary scholar, Sorouja's research-creation practice undertakes a multimodal critical discourse analysis of all forms of media including adaptations of Shakespeare in Canada, and an intersectional approach to nineteenth-century archival and narrative-based communication structures and applications, and their present-day manifestations in, among other areas, nation, memory, and identity in performance. Moll's areas of research include the oral histories of mixed-race identity; Indigenous and non-Indigenous relationship rebuilding practices and education as meaningful and sustainable; and exploring and creating incubatory spaces in which transgression, enunciation, ambiguity, and emancipation can be explored through performance, theatre, creative writing, and research practices.

As an award-winning author, Sorouja's writing has been profiled on CBC Radio and published in *The Globe and Mail, Toronto Star, Canadian Theatre Review,* as well as academic and literary journals, and books. As a playwright and performance artist, Sorouja's work has been presented across Canada.